Perfecting Patient Journeys

Improving patient safety, quality, and satisfaction while building problem-solving skills

by

Judy Worth

Tom Shuker

Beau Keyte

Karl Ohaus

Jim Luckman

David Verble

Kirk Paluska

Todd Nickel

Lean Enterprise Institute
Cambridge, MA, USA
lean.org

Version 1.0
December 2012

Lean Enterprise Institute

ISBN: 978-1-934109-36-6
Design by Thomas Skehan

Lean Enterprise Institute
215 First Street, Suite 300
Cambridge, MA 02142
617-871-2900 • fax: 617-871-2999 • lean.org

*See together. Learn together.
Act together.*

Acknowledgments

If, as the proverb goes, it takes a village to raise a child, then it takes a virtual village to produce a guide like this one. This is another way of saying that it's not possible to thank personally everyone who had a hand in bringing this guide to publication. However, we would like to acknowledge the contributions of the following individuals and groups:

Sam Watson, senior vice president patient safety and quality, MHA Keystone Center, Michigan Health & Hospital Association, recognized the need to integrate lean thinking and practices within the Keystone Emergency Room Collaborative and invited us to participate. It also was at Sam's request and with Keystone support that we developed the initial draft of this guide to support our work with the ER Collaborative. And, finally, Sam graciously accepted our request to provide the *Foreword* to this book, providing a context that anchors it in the inevitable and unpredictable future of healthcare delivery in the United States.

Brittany Bogan, Steven Levy, Kimberly Sepulvado, and other staff members of the MHA Keystone Center provided moral and logistical support as we piloted the use of this material with more than 65 hospitals over the four years of the ER Collaborative.

The members of the ER Collaborative teams who took this journey with us provided valuable feedback based on their experiences using the guide and applying the thinking and tools presented in the guide.

John Shook, CEO of Lean Enterprise Institute and our former partner, helped develop many of the ideas included in this guide as an outgrowth of work that contributed to the LEI publication, *Mapping to See*. We thank John for his belief in this project throughout this endeavor and for pushing us to walk the walk, continuously improving the draft as it moved through its many versions.

George Taninecz, our editor, spent considerably more hours than he anticipated helping us hammer this into a readable, cohesive, and consistent whole all the while retaining his patience and his sense of humor.

Thomas Skehan, our designer, made the guide more readable with his careful attention to the layout of the many maps, tables, sidebars, and the overall text.

Jane Bulnes-Fowles, director of learning materials at Lean Enterprise Institute, kept her laser eye on the potential audience for this guide and kept refocusing us on their requirements.

Dr. John Toussaint, CEO, and Helen Zak, president and COO, of The ThedaCare Center for Healthcare Value, reviewed multiple versions of the manuscript for this guide, offering valuable suggestions for fine-tuning the language and concepts for the broader healthcare audience. They also made it possible for us to circulate excerpts from the guide at the Third Annual Lean Healthcare Transformation Summit to get feedback prior to completion of the guide

Multiple other reviewers read one or more versions of the manuscript, encouraging us to proceed with the project because they recognized the value and challenged us to bring clarity to pages where we ran the risk of writing for ourselves, not our audience. We are grateful for all of their contributions to the final product.

We hope you will find it valuable as you work to improve the quality, safety, and efficiency of patient care.

The Authors

Foreword

Healthcare is undergoing the most significant change most of us have ever experienced. Patients have growing treatment options, and the tide of change in how healthcare is financed may well improve access and affordability. For those who provide care—physicians, nurses, and other health professionals—there are new pressures for not only improving the quality and safety of care delivery, but the efficiency as well. Likewise, those who lead healthcare organizations, those that pay for healthcare, employers, insurers, and the government all have to reimagine how to organize, pay for, and provide care.

Much hope is placed on the use of technology to address any number of woes in healthcare, from improving efficiency to patient safety. This is not surprising, as technology has been a significant part of advances in medicine. Many now hope that technology can turn the tide in the transformation of healthcare. But beliefs and behaviors are the root of transformation; technology merely enables, facilitates, and hastens change. As it stands, we have a healthcare delivery system that is unaffordable, inefficient, and sometimes downright dangerous. It is in need of true transformation. At the heart of transforming care we need to tap into the wisdom of those delivering care and equip them with the means to propagate the kind of change necessary to yield a new healthcare delivery system.

Dr. Avedis Donabedian, the father of quality improvement in healthcare, gave us a model to use when confronting how to improve care delivery. He suggested that we think about care in terms of structure, process, and outcomes. This framework allows us to apply science to make change. But applying science alone does not yield sustainable change.

Any of us leading change initiatives find some individuals ripe for change and laggards that fight us all the way. The majority between wait to see if it is real improvement or simply a fad. Their inaction—fearing change or new ways or fearing the loss of what they know—is driven by behaviors and beliefs (culture).

A fundamental part of our current culture is tied to how we have isolated, encapsulated, and segregated the how, what, who, when, and where of patient care. Everyone is keenly aware of the silos and talks about breaking them down, but applying science alone will not overcome these barriers. At the end of the day, we must apply science and address culture in order to make truly sustainable change.

Perfecting Patient Journeys and the approach it advocates of value-stream improvement bring together both the scientific and cultural components needed to begin transforming healthcare delivery. This book has its roots in a project with the MHA Keystone Center for Patient Safety & Quality. The MHA Keystone Center brought together hospitals in the state of Michigan to pursue improvements with unprecedented collaboration for expedited results. Over the past decade, we have applied both science and culture change to produce an environment that looks for prevention of harm and engages clinicians, administrators, and other members of the healthcare team. Most important, we have achieved results, such as driving infection rates to zero among participating hospitals. It is the combination of culture and science that creates the environment for sustainable change.

As we look ahead to the needed transformation of how we deliver healthcare, there are difficult questions to ask about how we care for patients and how patients wish to receive their care. In some cases we have clinical evidence that supports changes in how we deliver care. Yet in other instances either there is not an evidence base or the changes are not clinical in nature. So while we set forth to change culture and enact change, we also must gather evidence and continue to rely on Dr. Donabedian's structure, process, and outcome. This is the approach we took at the MHA Keystone Center as we conducted a project of changing processes in emergency departments across the state.

Value-stream improvement (VSI) served as the basis for our ED improvement effort. Because it was impractical to bring teams from more than 70 emergency departments to a three-day lean session or to deploy lean consultants on-site at each hospital, the authors of *Perfecting Patient Journeys* applied an innovative method: Small teams attended collaborative learning sessions and then returned to their hospitals to engage and coach the rest of their staffs. This process of socialization engaged the physicians and nurses at each emergency department, giving them the science necessary to make change and shaping their beliefs about their own abilities to influence their work environments and change their cultures.

The authors created a field guide to support the training used during the collaborative sessions and, thus, provided attendees the means to train their colleagues. That field guide became the basis for *Perfecting Patient Journeys*. Written in a clear manner without excessive lean jargon or terminology, this book presents the value-stream improvement approach, which simultaneously blends the ability to change structure and process while changing culture.

I hope that as you read and use *Perfecting Patient Journeys* it serves as a guide to support change in your organization. There is no circumventing the hard work of transformation. By engaging the clinicians, supporting them with the right tools, and, most importantly, listening to their wisdom, you will find a path toward sustainable transformation.

—Sam R. Watson
  Senior VP for Patient Safety and Quality, Michigan Health & Hospital Association
  Executive Director, MHA Keystone Center for Patient Safety & Quality
  November 2012

Contents

Chapter 5: Measuring the Future State and Planning for Change

- Create a way to measure the future state
- Establish goals and actions
- Learn how to conduct experiments
- Communicate and delegate actions
- Prepare to manage change

Chapter 6: Establishing Project Management

- Ensure execution of your improvement plan
- Develop a process to monitor progress
- Focus your progress checks and reviews
- Communicate and display progress
- Reinforce PDCA

Chapter 7: Keeping Your Improvement Project on Track

- Identify performance to plan, assess impact, and maximize learning
- Make adjustments
- Learn and apply lean problem-solving methods
- Establish roles for checks and reviews

Chapter 8: Moving Forward—From Projects and Events to Consistent Practice

- Conduct end-of-project review and reflection
- Learn how to stabilize and sustain
- Continue to solve problems
- Address organizational and cultural barriers
- Share your learnings
- Seize the next opportunity

Appendix: Value-Stream Improvement Roles

Glossary

About the Authors

About the Lean Enterprise Institute and the Healthcare Value Network

Introduction

How often have you and your colleagues debated ways to improve something but failed to agree on what needed to be fixed or how to fix it, or worse, knowingly picked a solution without sufficient buy-in and support—and then suffered through a difficult and unproductive change? For groups working in healthcare to make effective change *together*—change that produces wanted and/or needed improvements—there must be agreement on the problem, on its importance to your organization and the care it provides, and on a set of solutions.

Perfecting Patient Journeys presents a method for healthcare providers to:

- Identify and agree on a problem,

- Collaboratively develop a *set of potential solutions* to the problem,

- Experiment in order to find the best solution to address the problem,

- Communicate, share, and learn from the results.

If it were only that simple, you would not need a guide.

The method—value-stream improvement—is based on lean thinking, which has been around for decades and had its origins in manufacturing in Japan. Lean thinking has spread worldwide and throughout virtually every product and service business, including healthcare. Lean thinking looks at the delivery of services or goods as a stream of activities in which, ideally, all participants along that stream are creating value that meets customer (e.g., patient) needs and minimizes activities that do not create or add value.

Many in healthcare are new to lean and this concept of "value streams." Others have become keenly aware in the past five to 10 years of its applicability to the challenges that confront healthcare organizations and providers today. Patient journeys travel through many health-care value streams, and the quality and efficiency of these journeys in most organizations is insufficient. Improving patient journeys requires intervention at the value-stream level.

Examining and working to improve healthcare value streams addresses problems affecting your organization now, and it also develops the skill sets and mindsets for a new way to work, manage, and lead. This guide presents a method for you and your colleagues to sort through the maze of problems within your function, unit, department, facility, or organization; establish priorities; and focus as a group on solving the right problems together. And by "you" we mean managers, staff, specialists, *and doctors* on the frontlines of healthcare. This guide also will help senior leadership support system-level improvements in their organizations, but it is primarily intended for those in direct contact with patients and/or the individuals who support their work.

For the past eight years, we have helped healthcare organizations learn how to make real and sustainable change using the value-stream improvement method and have helped healthcare providers develop an adaptive, problem-solving culture—one that focuses on preventing fires rather than constantly fighting them. Results at these organizations have included:

- Reduced the average length of stay (LOS) in a large emergency department by 30%,

- Reduced the number of patients who left without being seen (LWOBS) by 60% in the same hospital,

- Increased independently gathered customer (patient) satisfaction scores by 73%,

- Reduced operating-room changeover time, which increased the number of surgical procedures performed by 20%,

- Reduced annual staff turnover by as much as 67%.

Step-by-step in this guide, you and your colleagues will learn how to make incremental improvements *as a team* and begin to develop a new way of looking at problems (value-stream mapping) and a new way of solving problems (the scientific method). Gradually you'll overcome five shortcomings of most group problem solving:

1. Failure to get agreement on the problem to be solved,

2. Lack of a common process for discovering the underlying causes of the problem and building consensus for solutions,

3. Failure to take a systemic view of the problem and potential solutions,

4. Failure to see problem solving as an experimental process,

5. Inability to engage the people necessary for change, those who will design the experiments and evaluate their outcomes.

It is our hope that by patiently working through the steps in this guide, you will learn how to identify and select a problem in the performance of a specific value stream, define a project scope, create a shared understanding of what's occurring in the value stream, develop a shared vision of an improved future, and work together to make that vision a reality. You will understand that anything labeled "best practice" should be qualified with "right now." That is to say, it is the best practice you know right now. Tomorrow, or some other time in the future, there will be a better practice—there is always a better way, it just isn't known yet. And by continuing the search for the better practice and experimenting, you will develop a culture of true continuous improvement.

Value-stream improvement does not rely on huge training budgets or teams of consultants. But it does require a few key individuals to learn how to lead, engage, and champion the effort, as well as external lean coaches/facilitators if your organization is unfamiliar with the application of lean concepts. It involves intensive skills-building but includes little conventional training. It focuses on solving real organizational problems by those living with and working in the problems, but it still has formal connection to and support from senior leadership through a "champion" role and a leadership panel. And value-stream improvement does not assume that all your problems will be eliminated, but it does help your organization build capability to solve its own problems.

Most important, attacking your organization's problems with this method actively engages the people closest to the work and most knowledgeable about the problems to collectively develop workable solutions. And by doing so, they view problems and improvement in a new light and renew their commitment to providing safe, effective, efficient, and timely patient care.

—Judy Worth
  Tom Shuker
  Beau Keyte
  Karl Ohaus
  Jim Luckman
  David Verble
  Kirk Paluska
  Todd Nickel

Chapter 1
Team-Based Problem Solving and Learning for Continuous Improvement

This chapter will:

• Reveal a new way of looking at healthcare problems, as patient journeys and value streams.

• Present a team-based, project-oriented approach for solving healthcare problems.

• Help to identify a purpose for improvement in your organization.

• Identify team roles required for your initial improvement project.

• Help you define a problem linked to organizational purpose.

• Present a method to communicate your project and gain cooperation, commitment, and enthusiasm.

Chapter 1
Team-Based Problem Solving and Learning for Continuous Improvement

The Need to Improve Patient Journeys in Healthcare

Imagine that you have been invited to tour the Emergency Department (ED) of St. Luke's Hospital. As you enter you see about 30 people, some sitting in chairs and some standing. You learn that some are waiting to go into the ED, others are waiting for triage, and the rest are family members of those seeking treatment. A few patients, you are told, have been waiting for seven hours to see a doctor. One patient gasps for breath, prompting another person to run to the triage area for help, which finally arrives. Around the corner you see a group clustered at registration, where there is no privacy for a young woman who is crying and trying to explain why she needs to be seen.

You walk into the ED and see people sitting—patients on gurneys, doctors in front of computers, and family members in chairs. Others mingle about, standing and talking. There are no empty rooms. Two patients wait to be discharged. Family members stand in the walkway next to drawn curtains. A doctor yells at a nurse, "Why aren't the labs back yet?" The nurse makes a phone call, walks over to a clipboard, and yells back, "They're here. They've been here for 15 minutes." Outside one curtained room, a phlebotomist waits with a tray of tubes to draw blood, and behind her a radiologic technologist waits for the same patient. From another curtain emerges an angry man, who yells, "I want a doctor in here now. My daughter has been here for 45 minutes!" Staff members occasionally rush to and from patient rooms to computer stations, and then they stand and wait until the next rush.

Back outside, an ambulance arrives and everyone stops and refocuses their energy on getting a critically injured patient into a treatment area. Still in the patient area, 25 minutes later, are the two patients waiting to be discharged.

The many problems in the St. Luke's ED delay, impair, and endanger patients' journeys through the ED. Until healthcare organizations address problems as patient journeys—in emergency departments and elsewhere throughout their facilities—they will struggle to reduce or eliminate their problems.

A patient's journey can involve travel through one or more value streams in your organization. A value stream consists of all the activities or processes necessary to deliver care that meets the patient's needs. In the real world, your world, a value stream includes activities that create value as well as those that do not create value. For example, if a patient spends 15 minutes on a gurney in a hallway waiting for imaging, the time spent waiting does not provide value. Identifying, understanding, and improving value streams in your organization—not as isolated tasks but as a flow of interconnected, interdependent activities and processes—is the starting point to perfecting patient journeys.

The Value-Stream Improvement Method

This guide will help healthcare organizations improve patient journeys through value streams and simultaneously build the problem-solving capabilities of individuals working in those value streams. The guide is intended for healthcare professionals whose roles and responsibilities include ensuring the organization's ability to deliver safe, high-quality, cost-effective care, and to deliver all the support services for the efficient and cost-effective delivery of that care. Such roles may include but are not limited to chief of medicine, VP of nursing, operations-improvement coordinator, VP of business transformation, the head of quality, and clinic manager.

In writing *Perfecting Patient Journeys*, we are speaking to people who want improvement and change across their organizations—improved patient safety and quality and improved work life for those delivering care and providing support services. These also are leaders who recognize that the individuals involved in delivering care know the most about their work and are the key to changing and improving work and value streams.

The improvement method presented in *Perfecting Patient Journeys*—value-stream improvement (VSI)—focuses on changing a specific value stream that has a problem (or problems) in performance and needs improvement. The VSI method will be introduced into your organization through a project or series of projects. As your organization gains experience with VSI concepts and techniques, they will become part of daily work and will eventually transition to a new way of continuously improving the delivery of patient care. All involved—eventually that should be everyone in your organization—will develop their abilities to continuously improve the value streams in which they work, and continuously develop a new way of looking at and doing work. VSI provides everyone the opportunity to practice integrating improvement work with doing work. And as projects are conducted throughout an organization and the method repeated, improvement work becomes an integral part of the work routine rather than something extra or a one-time event.

Your organization faces many value streams with many problems. Because this method ensures that improvement efforts are made in the context of an entire value stream, no part of the value stream makes progress at the expense of the rest. What results is a performance that is more effective and efficient across the entire value stream. And because every value stream is different, every value-stream improvement project will be different, even for similar value streams within your organization. However, the VSI method and techniques are consistent value stream to value stream—learned and applied continuously. And because the approach is consistent and applicable to any and all value streams, you will be developing people who are able to solve any problem in your organization that affects patient journeys.

Value-stream improvement projects consist of three phases (see *Improvement Phases of a VSI Project* on page 4). Initial projects typically include a preparation phase that defines the problems to be addressed. This occurs in a workshop of usually three days that, through defining current and target conditions, creates agreement about the nature of those problems and potential ways to address them. This is followed by the actual improvement phase of 60 to 120 days, running rapid learning experiments, and implementing changes that help improve the performance of the value stream. Lean terminology refers to these changes as "countermeasures" because, unlike "solutions" that infer a permanent fix, a countermeasure encourages continuous improvement of the system not just a list of problems to tackle.

In changing and improving value streams you will learn much about your work and about lean problem-solving techniques. This learning will be documented through a series of reflections that occur at the end of each phase. During these reflections you and the improvement team will be asked to assess how successful you have been in communicating proposed changes, eliciting feedback and input, and sharing what you've learned with leadership, stakeholders, and other parts of your organization. It is this learning that will embed sustainable continuous improvement across the value stream.

From the moment a value stream has been selected for improvement, from agreeing on the scope to mapping through implementation, actual changes must be made by the people doing the work and managing the work in the value stream. This is the hallmark of lean thinking: Frontline staff take ownership of the value-stream problems. Management takes responsibility for establishing the problem-solving infrastructure, defining goals, providing staff time for the improvement work, and mentoring staff to implement initiatives that support strategic objectives.

Improvement Phases of a VSI Project

Phase	Description	Content/Topics
1. Select problem and scope project	Leadership will define the broad organizational need for a project, grasp the situation (how the problem is affecting the organization), describe it for others, and define the purpose for improvement as well as the scope of the project.	• Problem statement • Lean value proposition • Socialization • Elevator speech
2. Map and plan (value-stream mapping workshop)	Value-stream stakeholders dig deeper to uncover the real value-stream problems and their underlying causes. A core team (the improvement team) develops a current-state value-stream map that shows the inputs and outputs for a value stream and all the steps involved. The team analyzes the current state, identifies and prioritizes problems, and proposes countermeasures that address the most likely causes in the form of a future-state map (how this value stream should work to meet performance requirements). Finally, team members translate their future-state vision into specific goals (hypotheses) and actions (experiments).	• Current-state value-stream map • Future-state value-stream map • Goals and action plans • Socialization
3. Make changes (implement) and reflect	The team conducts a series of experiments and tests the changes, and then measures and checks the results of the changes. As problems occur (experiments fail to deliver expected results, or new barriers surface), team members adjust their actions and regularly communicate findings to all stakeholders, including leadership. Reflection ensures that the learning is thorough and made explicit, enabling sustainable continuous improvement.	• Measuring results • Visual management • Problem solving • Conducting reviews and checks • Respect • Transitioning to continuous improvement • Socialization

Value-stream improvement is based on the scientific method, which provides the foundation for many approaches to problem solving. Throughout this guide you will see this problem-solving method referred to in the form of the plan-do-check-act (PDCA) cycle, also known as plan-do-study-act or -adjust (PDSA). PDCA corresponds with VSI project phases and the actions that are taken to address specific problems and improve performance (see *PDCA and Improvement Steps* on page 6).

As a healthcare professional you are already familiar with the PDCA method even though you may not recognize the terminology. PDCA forms the basis for all clinical care provided to patients who come to you with some type of problem.

1. Clinical care begins with assessment of the patient's condition leading to a diagnosis and plan of care (grasp the situation and plan). The treatment plan is a hypothesis about what is wrong with the patient and what will make the patient better.

2. The next step is treatment for the diagnosed problem (do). Treatment is the experiment to see if the hypothesis is correct.

3. Followup with the patient determines if the treatment is working (check). The patient's improvement, or lack thereof, as observed in followup tells you whether the experiment succeeded or failed.

4. Additional action (act) is taken as needed.

Just as PDCA in a clinical setting is applicable even though every patient is different, PDCA in an improvement setting is applicable even though every value stream is different. Changes are driven by conditions in the value stream, and value-stream improvement steps occur as you and team:

1. Make a detailed assessment of the current state and the need for change;

2. Develop a plan to implement change through a series of experiments;

3. Implement change and measure the results;

4. Take appropriate followup action.

**PDCA and
Improvement Steps**

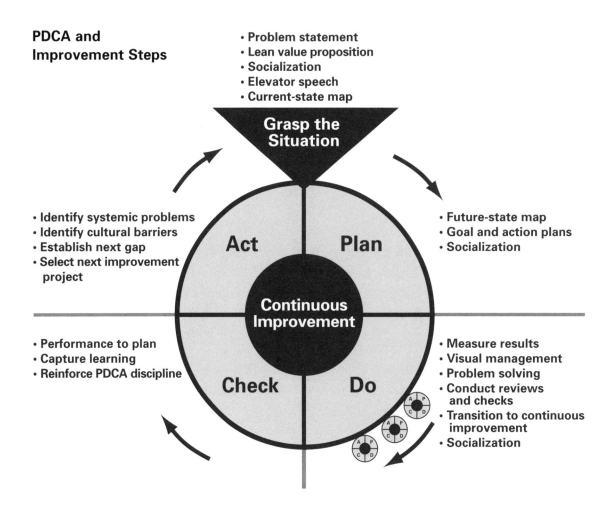

- Problem statement
- Lean value proposition
- Socialization
- Elevator speech
- Current-state map

Grasp the Situation

- Identify systemic problems
- Identify cultural barriers
- Establish next gap
- Select next improvement project

Act

Plan

- Future-state map
- Goal and action plans
- Socialization

Continuous Improvement

- Performance to plan
- Capture learning
- Reinforce PDCA discipline

Check

Do

- Measure results
- Visual management
- Problem solving
- Conduct reviews and checks
- Transition to continuous improvement
- Socialization

One aspect of the VSI method is unique to lean thinking, and that is the belief that "no problem is a problem." This is another way of saying that if there are no problems to solve, there are also no opportunities to improve. Continuous improvement is based on the assumption that, no matter how good things are right now, they can always be better.

The lean definition of a problem is a gap between where things are now and where they are supposed to be or where you would like them to be. Lean thinking requires that you recognize there is a gap (a problem), no matter how insurmountable or controversial it may seem. Only by identifying and working on that gap can you close it and make genuine, continuous, and sustainable improvement (see *Defining a Problem* on page 7).

Defining a Problem

The first step in problem solving is to *define the problem*. In lean thinking, problems are defined as gaps between the way things are and the way they should be. In other words, a problem is any performance other than desired performance at any given time.[1]

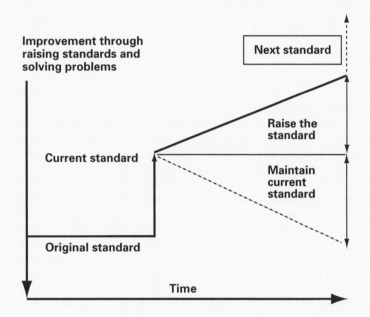

A problem is any performance other than desired performance at any given time.

One way to look at problems (i.e., gaps) is to think in terms of standards. A gap can exist between current performance and an established standard or a new standard that you are attempting to achieve. Consider a hypothetical length-of-stay (LOS) benchmark of 2 hours. If your current performance is averaging 4.5 hours, you have a gap of 2.5 hours. The problem is that the length of stay is too long. Whether you've slowed down and are not hitting the mark or have never been able to achieve the 2-hour standard, you have defined a gap (problem).

A problem also can be unwanted variation in performance even when average performance appears acceptable. When even a single out-of-specification event is a problem (e.g., failure to follow proper handwashing techniques before touching a patient), the gap exists between any number of events and no events.

1. John Shook, *Managing to Learn*, (Cambridge, MA, Lean Enterprise Institute, 2008).

Why Improve (Purpose)?

You now have a method to improve—value-stream improvement and PDCA problem solving. To get maximum and lasting impact from your improvement efforts, however, everyone involved in that effort must adhere to a common *purpose* and work on a problem(s) that links to that purpose.

Defining a common purpose begins with clearly identifying a need in your organization:

- Customer service (e.g., reduced length of stay),

- Clinical quality and safety (e.g., reduced number of patients who acquire infections while in the hospital),

- Business (e.g., increased revenue or market share; in a hospital this could translate to freed-up resources that can be devoted to patient care, innovation, etc.).

Organizational needs occur at various levels (unit, department, facility, network) and are driven by many factors, such as outside mandates, a newspaper exposé of long wait times, competitors' superior performances, and/or government regulations.

Once an organizational need is recognized, the next step is to identify a problem with a specific function (e.g., Lab, Radiology, Surgery) or value stream associated with the need. Identifying where problems are likely occurring is leadership's responsibility as part of strategy deployment, a senior-leadership process of identifying goals and objectives for the entire organization. For example, many hospitals must reduce unplanned readmissions within 30 days in order to retain federal reimbursements from the Centers for Medicare & Medicaid Services. If unplanned readmissions rise, leadership will work to identify functions or departments that have a problem that could be causing unplanned readmissions.

Learning Collaboratives

Organizations working on projects may opt to use a learning-collaborative approach, which brings together small teams from various organizations, or from different value streams within the same organization, on a regular basis to receive periodic instruction, draft work products, identify countermeasures, and report on their progress and learnings.

In this guide, we illustrate the value-stream improvement method at a fictitious hospital, St. Luke's. The events at St. Luke's—from kickoff of its initial project to ongoing improvement activities—will show application of the VSI method within a healthcare facility, but the method can similarly be applied in a clinic, physician practice, rehab center, skilled nursing facility, etc., or as a collaborative of multiple organizations (see *Learning Collaboratives* on page 8).

St. Luke's leadership identified a common purpose as improving the performance of its Emergency Department (ED) value stream. Leadership chose the ED value stream based on the following criteria, which are recommended for selection decisions, especially for initial projects:

- Problem with performance that links to a compelling business, clinical, or customer-service need;

- Too many resources consumed and/or significant quality, cost, or delivery problems;

- Workflow that can be identified and mapped, process by process, with defined scope and performance metrics;

- Worthwhile investment of time and effort to improve.

St. Luke's leadership also agreed to dedicate resources for the improvement effort. They believed they could improve the ED's performance in delivering patient care, and they recognized that the ED project could provide an opportunity to experiment with building problem-solving capabilities.

St. Luke's Hospital Purpose—Improve Emergency Department Performance

St. Luke's is a medium-sized hospital with 250 beds and an Emergency Department (ED) that handles approximately 80,000 patients a year. The ED continues to struggle with long queues in the ED waiting room for "walk-in" patients with lower acuity levels (acuity 3–5). The higher-acuity patients (acuity 1–2) and those arriving by ambulance are moved into exam rooms immediately.

The staff is experiencing higher than normal turnover, and staff members appear overburdened with the ED processes. The executive administration of the hospital also is very concerned the ED could lose significant market share in the future due to the improvement of ED performance at two competing regional hospitals. As a result, other hospital services, e.g., Surgery and Radiology, also would lose business.

Who Is Involved (Improvement Team)?

Before St. Luke's or your organization can define a problem, it's important to decide who needs to define the problem? With the VSI method there are two major objectives:

1. To solve actual problems (close gaps),

2. To build capability (learn how to solve problems *as a team* through rapid experiments, and be able to apply this approach to problems in the future).

Meeting these objectives requires a *team approach*, one in which members define and solve problems together. A successful project requires clearly defined team roles and responsibilities for people involved in the improvement and those leading the improvement process. *Perfecting Patient Journeys* will guide individuals in the following four roles:

- *Lean champion* is a member of the organization's senior leadership team. He or she serves as the link between the leadership group that initiates the project and the project team. The lean champion is an advocate for the use of lean principles and tools in addressing a problem(s). The champion plays a key role in scoping the project, kicking off the project, removing barriers encountered by the improvement team, and ensuring accountability for project completion.

- *Lean facilitator* functions as an internal facilitator and coach through the life of the project. Typically this role is filled by someone with lean experience and expertise and frequently drawn from an organization's quality-improvement, process-improvement, continuous-improvement, or lean six sigma group. In organizations with no previous lean experience, this role may be filled by someone from the organizational development function.

- *Value-stream owner* assumes overall responsibility for the performance of the value stream designated for improvement. In a value stream with clear departmental boundaries (e.g., the value stream for emergency care), the department manager is typically the value-stream owner. For value streams that go across departmental boundaries (e.g., the value stream for in-patient care), leadership may need to designate an owner who interacts with all departments involved in delivering or supporting the delivery of in-patient care.

- *Improvement team* is a small multidisciplinary group of people directly involved in the work of the value stream as well as suppliers and customers of the value stream. Seven to 12 team members will draft current-state and future-state maps for the value stream, prioritize problems to be addressed in the first phase of the project, develop an implementation plan, involve others in running rapid learning experiments and implementing process improvements, and keep everyone who works in the value stream engaged and informed.

Some improvement projects also include a physician lean champion for the improvement of clinical value streams and/or a leadership panel to oversee the project. A leadership panel also may be desirable when an organization is so large and complex that only a portion of the organization's senior leadership needs to be engaged on an ongoing basis. (For more details on improvement roles, see page 149.)

As organizations undertake multiple improvement projects, these roles and their efforts will need to be linked to strategic priorities. Doing so helps ensure that your organization does not take on too many improvement projects or have conflicting projects, and that executives and staff are not spread too thin (e.g., repeatedly tapping the same people because of their proven skills and belief in the method). Connecting projects to the group that oversees strategic priorities also can prevent an overlap of projects and competition for resources (e.g., attempting a project in a department that is in the middle of relocating to new space). In larger organizations this connection is often made through a steering committee, which includes senior leaders or their direct reports. The lean champion or the director/ executive to whom he or she reports is generally a member of this group.

Project leadership requires leading by example and engaging others to build alignment and support. In addition to embracing the roles as defined, people filling the key roles must have strong interpersonal skills and be:

- Good listeners, learners, teachers, and coaches;

- Able to work well with others;

- Respected by their fellow team members;

- Good communicators;

- Able to adjust their style to the audience, utilizing appropriate methods to solicit input, solve problems, and make decisions.

The Problem and the Problem Statement

What problem will your team address? What is the gap that needs to be closed and where is it located? To ensure clarity and gain consensus around the problem, develop a *problem statement* that briefly describes the current situation (the gap) in measurable terms and its impact on customers (e.g., patients), staff, and the organization. The problem statement helps everyone understand what problem is under discussion and agree that the problem needs addressed. It also explains how closing the gap will benefit the various stakeholders.

A problem statement is usually drafted by the leadership panel or the value-stream owner, the lean champion, and the lean facilitator. The overall improvement team, along with individuals who work in the value stream and other stakeholders, review the draft problem statement and provide feedback. Stakeholders must see the connection to their own work —"Why am I involved?"—in order to buy in. Approaching problems as a team requires buy-in from all roles and at all stages, without which your efforts will lack direction and cohesion, making problem solving more difficult. Moreover, if team members are not aligned around the problem statement, they are less likely to continue to improve the performance after the initial problem is solved.

If the problem is defined too narrowly or a solution is identified too early by leadership or one individual, the team may have no choice but to go along with the stated problem and/or solution. If this individual is in a position of authority, the team is unlikely to challenge either the individual's definition of the problem or proposed solution. That can shut down the voices of team members and cause them to overlook underlying causes of the problem and offer a "blanket solution." Either approach limits the team's ability to compare multiple options and ultimately reach consensus on the best course of action.

Note that consensus does not necessarily mean everyone must agree on every particular of the team's analysis of the problem or the proposed solution. Visibility of the problem allows a team to see together, learn together, and act together, despite their individual differences. Visibility is achieved through "go see" activities (see *Conducting a Go-See* at right). Looking with all eyes, the team begins the process of agreeing on a problem to solve.

Conducting a Go-See

Go-see activities help to build consensus around the problem. Sometimes called "going to gemba" (a Japanese term for going to "the actual place or actual thing"), go-see refers to visiting the place where work is being performed and observing firsthand what is happening. Taiichi Ohno, one of the fathers of lean thinking, once observed, "Data are highly regarded, but I consider facts to be even more important."[2] And the facts of a situation can best be observed where the problem is actually happening—not in a conference room or at a desk.

Before you draft your problem statement, you (the lean champion, the lean facilitator, the value-stream owner if identified, and the leadership panel) will benefit by doing a brief 30-minute walk through the value stream to see firsthand what's actually happening on a typical day. (Keep in mind that a typical day may not take into account the differences that occur between weekday and weekend operations and on different shifts in a 24/7 health-care operation.) What you see and what you hear as you talk to the people working in the value stream and perhaps its customers may give you a very different view of the problem and the underlying causes.

These tips will help you efficiently and respectfully gather facts during a go-see activity:

- Give advance notice (at least a day) to the people working in the area you plan to see. Explain the purpose of your visit (e.g., to see firsthand what the patient and staff experience is like). And advise them that the visitors may ask a few questions to help them better understand what they are seeing.

- Break into teams of two or three persons, and assign each team to observe different parts of the value stream or to begin at different vantage points in the value stream. Remind them of the focus for this go-see.

- Observe without intruding to get a read on the environment, the way the work flows, and any apparent problems.

- Ask people working in the area (and patients and family members, as appropriate) to describe their work (or experiences) and struggles: e.g., "What makes a good or bad day for you? Why? What is your understanding of what makes it good or bad? What do you think is going on? How long does it take to progress the patient/paperwork to the next step? Why? How do these problems impact the patient and colleagues?"

- As appropriate, follow a patient through an entire journey (or multiple patients through different parts of the value stream).

- At the end of the go-see, reconvene and briefly share your observations.

- After this first go-see, revisit your problem statement and see if what you described corresponds to what you observed during your visit to the gemba. Revise the problems statement as needed.

2. Taiichi Ohno, *Toyota Production System: Beyond Large-Scale Production*, English translation (New York, Productivity Press, 1988.)

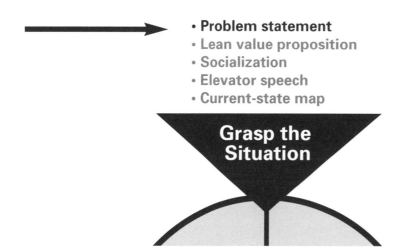

- **Problem statement**
- Lean value proposition
- Socialization
- Elevator speech
- Current-state map

Grasp the Situation

Identifying the problem to address and developing a problem statement are part of "grasp the situation," which begins your team's entry into the PDCA cycle. When you are developing problem statements, your task is to describe the observable facts of the situation—what you see and hear—not to come to conclusions or offer solutions. In addition to arriving to solutions too quickly, there also is a tendency to bring analysis into the problem statement. Analysis argues why something is or why it occurred. The opportunity for analysis will come when you break down the problem. For now, your problem statement should be limited to what you actually know and can confirm. Problems should be based on facts, which are observable. Therefore, when you see reasons or assumptions in problem statements, step back to the facts.

And be aware of "would-be" problems. Problem statements with the words "lack of ____," "not enough___," or "inadequate ____," are "would be" problem statements. They suggest that if there were some or more of "___," there "would be" no problem. If you are struggling to define problems as gaps, one way to come to an appropriate problem statement is to start with one of these would-be problem statements, and ask yourself "what will having ___ solve?" Then ask, "Is that the real problem?"

The simple exercise of crafting a problem statement can be challenging because stating a problem as a gap without suggesting a solution is not common practice. Many organizations say they reward "problem solving," which has the unintended consequence of encouraging employees to take swift action. Unwittingly, such organizations reflect a culture with a bias for action over a careful consideration of the situation and the consequences (intended and unintended) of proposed action. In such cases, problems are stated with an implied solution. Real analysis of the problem is limited, and the possibility of multiple causes and multiple solutions is ignored. As a consequence, many of these solutions result in more waste.

Here are some tips for writing a good problem statement:

- Describe the current situation (the gap) in measurable terms and its impact on your customers (e.g., patients), staff, and your organization.
- Describe how closing the gap would benefit those stakeholders.
- Describe how closing the gap would address an organizational need.

St. Luke's Problem Statement

St. Luke's identified its problems and linked them to organizational need:

Our ED faces long waits for low-acuity patients, high staff turnover, and potential loss of market share to other hospitals in the region, which promise a "door to doc" time of 30 minutes and a visit time of 2.5 hours for most patients. Reducing our patient LOS in the ED would increase our patients' satisfaction with our care and keep them safer, make work more satisfying for our staff members who work in the ED, and make it less likely that patients will abandon our hospital to seek care from our competitors.

Building Cooperation, Commitment, and Enthusiasm with Socialization

Getting stakeholders personally vested in solving the problem and working together toward addressing larger organizational issues requires socialization, a cycle of communication, modification, and consensus building. This practice gives each stakeholder an opportunity to be heard.

Since lean problem solving may be new to your organization, the individuals leading the improvement effort should discuss what they're trying to achieve with socialization and how they will practice it (see *Getting the Most from Socialization* on page 17). Just as crafting a problem statement with all stakeholders at the same time is rarely feasible, socialization is not one big announcement. It occurs among smaller groups over time, and, in doing so, provides feedback on multiple realities (different groups and different people will react differently to what's presented to them based on their experiences and underlying assumptions).

Think of your problem statement as a work-in-progress during socialization. Your view of the situation may change. Keep in mind where you are with respect to your own understanding of the problem and what you are trying to get out of socializing it. You try to narrow and settle on a problem statement, and you use socialization to confirm what you know about the problem and solicit additional information from stakeholders:

• What do you know? (performance gap)—How can you confirm it?

• What do you need to know?—How can you learn it?

Socialize the draft problem-statement by:

1. Stating what you're trying to accomplish (including the purpose),

2. Narrowing the scope of the project to frame the discussion,

3. Describing the process you'll be using to focus the dialogue,

4. Inviting others to participate and give feedback (within the scope).

Consider the context in which the problem statement was developed, including the perspective and knowledge (at that time), and clearly communicate that context to each stakeholder. The more they understand that this is an evolutionary process with cycles of communication and modification, the more likely they will be drawn in and contribute. If stakeholders think of socialization as simply one-way communication, they will quickly tune you out.

As you put the draft problem statement before stakeholders, remember that you also are trying to learn how to improve your socialization practices. Reflect afterward on the following:

1. Was the dialogue constructive and helpful?

2. Was there appropriate contribution from all stakeholders?

3. Was there consensus?

4. What was learned?

5. What should change for the next effort?

Getting the Most From Socialization

We use the term "socialization" to describe how improvement teams communicate facts and plans, share ideas, and encourage feedback. Some healthcare organizations already on their lean journey and undertaking value-stream improvements may refer to this as "nemawashi," a Japanese term meaning a process of gaining acceptance and preapproval for proposals. Your organization may describe these practices as "vetting" or "gaining support and input." Use a term that reasonates within your organization.

Remember that socialization is more than simply providing information or building consensus. Answering the following questions can help you get the best results from socialization.

Productive dialogue	• What kind of feedback are you looking to receive? • What questions are you trying to answer? • What discussion topics do you want to avoid?
Contribution from key stakeholders	• Who needs to participate? • Should the method for engaging vary depending on the function or the type of contribution you expect? • Do you access colleagues at an existing meeting, a special meeting, in groups (what size?), or individually? • How much time will you need with each person?
Reaching consensus	• How will you confirm that agreement has been reached? Will you use a consensus-building technique, such as "agree-to-proceed" or "fist-to-five," to make consensus visible?* • Will you need followup sessions to communicate to all involved stakeholders afterward, especially if the original problem statement evolves as others contribute? • Should you build in the expectation for additional conversations?
Preparation	• Taking into account all the above, what is your plan for the process you will use? • What preparation is necessary to ensure your plan? • Have you determined what is likely to go wrong and added additional countermeasures to reduce the risk of such occurrences? • Are you clear on the roles and the assignments made to the facilitator, champion, and process owner?

*Agree-to-proceed and fist-to-five are techniques that offer participants the means to indicate the strength of their support for a proposed action and a means to reach a consensus.

Chapter 2:
Scoping Your Improvement Project

This chapter will help you and your team:

• **Identify participants for the improvement project.**

• **Select the value stream (or processes within a value stream) to target.**

• **Establish boundaries (what not to include so the project can be managed).**

• **Record key project characteristics, agreed to by all, in the value proposition.**

Chapter 2:
Scoping Your Improvement Project

Why Scope?

Now that your team has a problem statement that will serve as the driver for your value-stream improvement project, the next step is to determine your *project scope*. Scoping is the process of narrowing the focus to determine:

- Who needs to be involved (who needs to agree on the problem and its scope in order for the project to be successful)?

- Which value stream or value-stream activities will be targeted for improvement, and which departments or functions outside the value stream may need to be involved?

- What improvements are desired?

In Chapter 1, you began to "grasp the situation" related to your project, and by developing a problem statement you were able to get general consensus on the problem. In this chapter, scoping will refine that understanding and pull more stakeholders into the project. You also will develop a *lean value proposition* that further defines the project, and learn how to communicate the project via an *elevator speech*.

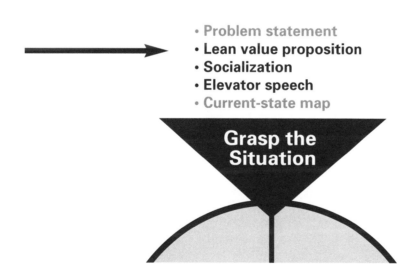

Participants in Scoping

Scoping is typically done by team leaders or managers who either have responsibility for performance of the value stream or whose departments or functions provide support to or are supported by the value stream. This group includes the lean champion, the value-stream owner, the lean facilitator, and other key leaders.

In our St. Luke's example, the ED manager and the medical director were involved in project scoping because they are responsible for the overall ED performance. In addition, managers from Radiology, Laboratory Services, and Patient Registration were included because their functions provide support to the ED and can have a profound impact on ED performance, both positive and negative. (Depending on the kind of problems that surfaced during go-see activities, the St. Luke's team might also have included representatives from Facilities Management, Ancillary Services, Pharmacy, and other departments.)

In addition to determining who needs to scope, you also need to determine how you will involve them. Will you bring the entire group together to do the scoping? Or will a smaller group (e.g., the lean champion, value-stream owner, and lean facilitator) draft a project scope and socialize it with the rest of the scoping group for review?

Do You Need a Medical Lean Champion?

You were asked in Chapter 1 to identify a lean champion. If your lean champion is not a physician—which is common—you might need to also consider a physician champion or physician project sponsor. Not every project will need a separate physician leadership role, but there are conditions where having a physician involved at a sponsor level can have a significant impact on the project's success:

Value stream: Are physicians directly involved in the value stream? Is there a clinical component to the problem associated with the value stream? Will physician participation in the improvement effort be required to really solve the problem? If so, physician buy-in is a must, and a medical lean champion can assist in developing it.

Culture: Are physicians employees of the hospital or contractors? How have past improvement efforts touched physicians? Is there a history of team problem solving among physicians, nurses, and administrative staff? In addition to the problem in question, what capabilities is your organization trying to build regarding working relationships with physicians?

Value Streams and Customers

You should already be familiar with the general concept of value streams and process improvement efforts. Although the terms "value stream" and "process" are frequently used interchangeably, there is an important distinction between the two. A value stream is a process that also includes a customer. The customer defines the purpose (i.e., the valued outcome/output) of the process:

$$process + customer\ (purpose) = value\ stream.$$

A clinical value stream consists of all the activities or processes necessary to deliver care that meets the patient's needs. Value-stream improvement includes process improvement, but it also can include improving the outcome/output to better meet customer requirements.

Think of value-stream improvement from two perspectives (either or both):

1. *Improving the effectiveness and efficiency of the resources and activities used to produce the outputs or outcomes.* For example, increasing the number of surgical procedures performed by reducing the Operating Room changeover time.

2. *Improving the effectiveness of the output/outcome relative to what the customer wants or needs.* For example, increasing patient satisfaction by reducing the wait time between patient arrival in the ED and the doctor's examination of the patient.

Whenever you focus on one of these perspectives, you need to maintain or improve the performance of the other as well. Whatever changes you incorporate to make a value stream more efficient, you must ensure that the end-use customer (the patient for clinical value streams as the ultimate user of what a clinical value stream produces) continues to receive an equal or better outcome.

Value-stream mapping is an essential tool for this because it helps make visible both of these perspectives. (You will learn more about value-stream mapping in Chapter 3.) By maintaining this dual focus, an organization is able to produce other needed results for all of its stakeholders (e.g., make a profit or stay within budget, improve staff satisfaction, and better serve the community).

Capture Scope in a Lean Value Proposition

The format you and your team will use to document your project scope is called a "value proposition" (see *St. Luke's Value Proposition* on page 23). You may recognize details in the value proposition that are similar to a SIPOC (supplier-input-process-output-customer) form. If a SIPOC form is used in your organization, it can provide some—but not all—of the details required for the value proposition. (For a blank value proposition template and other resources go to *lean.org/ppj*.)

The value proposition will help you and your team:

• Align the stakeholders around what will be included in addressing the problem,

• Identify the stakeholders who will be added to the project team and actively engaged in creating the current- and future-state value-stream maps,

• Identify additional stakeholders necessary to drive the implementation of the future state,

• Serve as an agreement—a proof of consensus—on the specific problem to be solved, and with the problem statement serve as authorization for the entire project.

The value proposition is not just a document to record discussions. It should be used to drive the discussions and reach consensus. The value proposition will be easier to complete and understand if you work through the template in the following sequence:

1. Name, Lean Champion, and Date

Record the name of the project and the lean champion. Give it a name that will help you and others describe the work. Include the date so that you can compare this product to future value propositions for this value stream.

2. Value-Stream Owner (and Project Owner if different from the value-stream owner)

The value-stream owner is responsible for the performance of the value stream. He/she understands and manages the improvement process, monitoring performance and leading the problem solving when performance is not on target. This does not mean that the value-stream owner directly supervises all the people who work in the process.

If your project involves a high-level, cross-functional value stream, such as in-patient care (not recommended for your first project because of the complexity involved), there may not be anyone specifically designated to manage the end-to-end value-stream performance. In that case, it is important that leadership designate a value-stream owner as soon as possible. Critical to the success of the project is to have the value-stream owner directly involved in creating the value proposition. If the value-stream owner has not participated in the initial draft, be sure to include him or her early in the socialization process.

St. Luke's Value Proposition

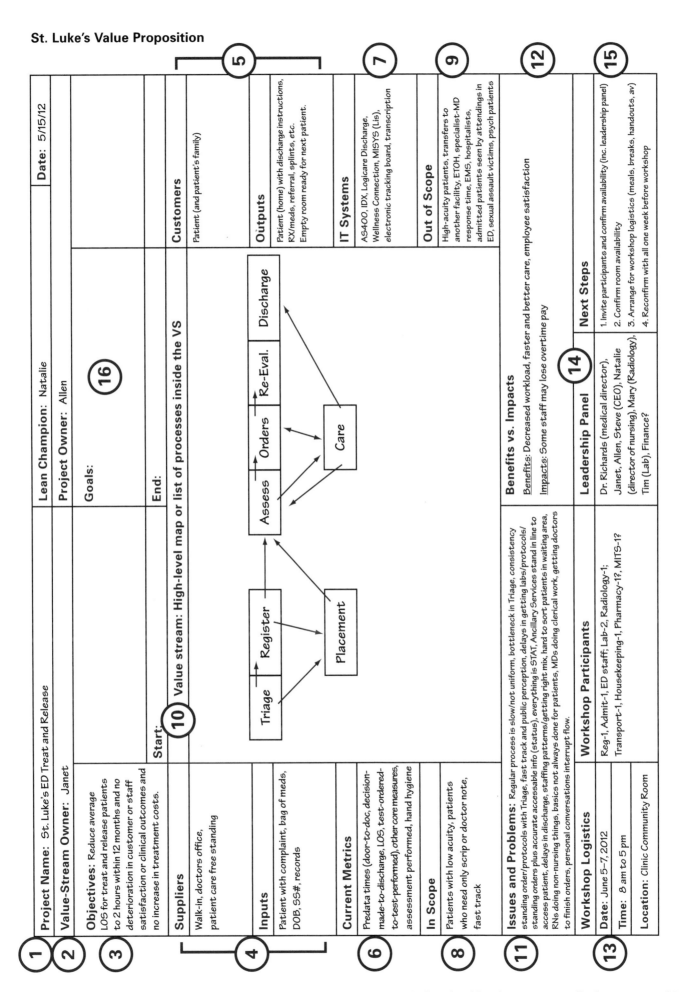

1. Project Name: St. Luke's ED Treat and Release — **Date:** 5/15/12

Lean Champion: Natalie

2. Value-Stream Owner: Janet

Project Owner: Allen

3. Objectives: *Reduce average LOS for treat and release patients to 2 hours within 12 months and no deterioration in customer or staff satisfaction or clinical outcomes and no increase in treatment costs.*

Goals: (16)

Start: / **End:**

4. Suppliers: Walk-in, doctors office, patient care free standing

5. Value stream: High-level map or list of processes inside the VS

Customers: Patient (and patient's family)

6. Inputs: Patient with complaint, bag of meds, DOB, SS#, records

Current Metrics: Predata times (door-to-doc, decision-made-to-discharge, LOS, test-ordered-to-test-performed), other core measures, assessment performed, hand hygiene

7. Outputs: Patient (home) with discharge instructions, RX/meds, referral, splints, etc. Empty room ready for next patient.

IT Systems: AS400, IDX, Logicare Discharge, Wellness Connection, MISYS (Lis), electronic tracking board, transcription

9. Out of Scope: High-acuity patients, transfers to another facility, ETOH, specialist-MD response time, EMS, hospitalists, admitted patients seen by attendings in ED, sexual assault victims, psych patients

8. In Scope: Patients with low acuity, patients who need only scrip or doctor note, fast track

10. Value stream: Triage → Register → Assess → Orders → Re-Eval. → Discharge; Care; Placement

11. Issues and Problems: Regular process is slow/not uniform, bottleneck in Triage, consistency standing order/protocols with Triage, fast track and public perception, delays in getting labs/protocols/standing orders plus accurate accessable info (status), everything is STAT, Ancillary Services stand in line to access patient, delays in discharge, staffing patterns/getting right mix, hard to sort patients in waiting area, RNs doing non-nursing things, basics not always done for patients, MDs doing clerical work, getting doctors to finish orders, personal conversations interrupt flow.

12. Benefits vs. Impacts:

Benefits: Decreased workload, faster and better care, employee satisfaction

Impacts: Some staff may lose overtime pay

14. Leadership Panel: Dr. Richards (medical director), Janet, Allen, Steve (CEO), Natalie (director of nursing), Mary (Radiology), Tim (Lab), Finance?

Next Steps:
1. Invite participants and confirm availability (inc. leadership panel)
2. Confirm room availability
3. Arrange for workshop logistics (meals, breaks, handouts, av)
4. Reconfirm with all one week before workshop

Workshop Participants: Reg-1, Admit-1, ED staff, Lab-2, Radiology-1; Transport-1, Housekeeping-1, Pharmacy-1?, MITS-1?

13. Workshop Logistics:

Date: June 5-7, 2012

Time: 8 am to 5 pm

Location: Clinic Community Room

There occasionally may be a separate project owner. For example, someone at the VP level may own the value stream but someone at the manager level, who is closer to the work, may be designated as project owner. For example, the VP of emergency services may be the value-stream owner but the ED manager may be a more appropriate choice to function as project owner.

3. Objectives

The objectives must be clear, measurable, and have specific time targets. In order to develop objectives, go back to your problem statement and think of the conditions that must be met to consider the problem solved. Start with the question, "How will you know?" That is, how will you know that the problem has been solved? What observable and/or measurable conditions would be present? Then incorporate these conditions as your objective.

St. Luke's Project Objective

St. Luke's problem statement was:

Our ED faces long waits for low-acuity patients, high staff turnover, and potential loss of market share to other hospitals in the region, which promise a "door to doc" time of 30 minutes and a visit time of 2.5 hours for most patients. Reducing our patient LOS in the ED would increase our patients' satisfaction with our care and keep them safer, make work more satisfying for our staff members who work in the ED, and make it less likely that patients will abandon our hospital to seek care from our competitors.

After reviewing the available ED performance data and the observations made during go-see activities, St. Luke's scoping group realized that 80% of their patients were discharged directly from the ED. Given the high volume of walk-ins and their impact on the overall length of stay (LOS) for the ED, the scoping group decided that the "treat and release" value stream (a subprocess of the ED value stream) was the one to address.

St. Luke's project objective is:

Reduce the average LOS for treat and release patients to 2 hours within 12 months with no deterioration in customer or staff satisfaction or clinical outcomes and no increase in treatment costs.

4. Suppliers and Inputs

Suppliers are the people or departments that provide the inputs that trigger work at the beginning of a value stream. Who are the suppliers for this value stream? What inputs do they provide? In clinical value streams, the input is usually a request for a service, or, in the case of the ED or Outpatient Care, a patient arrival. In our St. Luke's example, as in many healthcare processes, the supplier also is the customer.

However, if you have chosen to focus on a nonclinical value stream or only a small portion of a clinical value stream, your customers and suppliers are not likely to be the same. You also may want to include internal suppliers as well. For example, Lab and Radiology supply information in the form of reports to the ED value stream.

5. Customers and Outputs

Customers are the individuals or groups who use whatever outputs/outcomes the value stream produces. Frequently, you will have the patient as a customer, but you can have internal customers as well. For example, if your scope includes ED patients who are being admitted following their stay in the ED, then you will have both the patient and the hospital admissions as customers.

The customer of the process is not always the only or major beneficiary. For example, you may be working to improve the in-patient-care value stream. In doing so, you'll reduce waste experienced by nurses, which may allow them to see more patients or provide them more time per patient. The nurses are beneficiaries of an improved value stream, but not customers of the value stream.

6. Current Metrics

If current metrics are available for the value stream and for key segments, list them here. If not, you can determine what metrics you need to collect prior to value-stream mapping. (It's often sufficient to rely on the estimates of experienced staff members for mapping and then validate those estimates as you run experiments and trial improvements.)

7. IT Systems

List the systems that are used during the performance of the work within the value stream. It is common to categorize changes to IT systems as out-of-scope, but identifying them helps the team understand the complexity of the process as well as where you might have to go to find information.

8. In Scope

The term "in scope" defines what part of the value stream you want to address, if you don't plan to tackle the entire stream, and, for the purpose of value-stream mapping, where to start and stop (the first and last processes). In scope also will identify the duration of the project and access to investment or capital.

- *Whole or parts of a value stream*

  In one sense, your value stream has already been selected; it was selected by leadership when they identified it as a function that needed to be improved in relation to a customer service, clinical, and/or business need. However, the value stream may be more like a river than a stream, so big and complex that it will be difficult to know where to start or how to have impact. For that reason, you may want to address only a part of the entire value stream. Scoping will determine what part needs addressed.

  To help you decide what part of the value stream, go back and revisit your problem statement. Using available data and the observations you made during your go-see, identify what part of the value stream appears to be contributing most to the problems you observed. Or if you're trying to reach a new standard, identify what part of the value stream might be changed to help you reach the new level of performance.

  Think of scoping as slicing the process vertically to define which segments of the value stream will be addressed or horizontally to define the customer types/service families to be considered. For example, if you scope the value stream for in-patient surgery, you might decide that the bulk of your problems deal with patient scheduling and discharge, in which case you would limit your project to only those two segments. On the other hand, you might decide that the bulk of your problems are associated with elective surgery, so you would consider that as a separate stream from nonelective procedures. (Both of these would be considered smaller value streams that together make up the larger value stream of in-patient surgery.) If you chose only a portion of the value stream for your project, you may need to revise your project objective.

- *Value-stream processes*

  Once you've determined whether you want to address the entire value stream or some part of it, you need to determine the first and last processes in the value stream for the project. That may seem obvious, but because it has important consequences it needs careful consideration.

For example, if you're scoping a value stream for elective orthopedic surgery (e.g., total hip and total knee replacements), you need to decide when your value stream begins. Is it outside the hospital in the surgeon's office when your patient is listed for surgery? Is it when the physician calls the direct admit in? Is it when the physician says the patient is being admitted through the ED? Is it when the patient arrives at the registration desk at the hospital?

To complete scoping you need to determine, at a high level, the major processes in the value-stream. A process consists of the group of activities or steps that together produce a work product or result that is handed off to the next process in the value stream. For example, most in-patient value streams begin with the patient registration process.

If the entire scoping group is completing the value proposition together (recommended practice), the lean facilitator will lead them in exploring the value-stream processes as if through an adjustable lens—zoom control—to help them determine the scope for the project. A proper degree of zoom control should give you a scope that surfaces/reveals the performance issues that need to be addressed. Zoom out too far and the opportunities for improvement are not visible. Zoom in too much and you will lose the big picture amid all the details.

In addressing the number or level of details in the processes, remember that many more details will emerge about the process during the value-stream mapping phase. What may seem like a simple process when viewed from the enterprise level can appear quite involved when examined at the level of detail required for value-stream mapping.

Zoom control is not a one-time shot. Much like focusing a camera, the scope can be narrowed or expanded as a process/value stream is addressed. For example, critical activities or steps in a process may only become known when the actual improvement work begins, after which those steps will need to become part of the scope. For now, confine the improvement project to three to seven high-level processes in the value stream.

- *Timeframe*
As a starting point, consider an initial time frame for your project of one to two years. You will probably go through a phased series of three-month implementation projects or individual improvement events to get from where you are now to where you would like to be (where you want to be may change as you improve your value stream). Set your expectations and objectives for the project with this timeframe in mind.

- *Capital investments*

  Remember this effort is focused on addressing problems at the system level, which are complex and require cross-functional alignment. However, in determining your project scope you also need to consider the magnitude of the changes required by the organization and its capacity for change. For example, the question of changes to IT systems frequently arises. Because "no new capital" is usually a ground rule imposed by leadership for scoping a new project, you may be inclined to completely exclude IT system changes from the scope. However, some capital-equipment purchases, facility modifications, or other expenses may be necessary to support your desired improvements and may need to be budgeted.

  Consider leaving out changes that require new capital. There rarely is a silver bullet (or magic piece of equipment or IT application) that solves a problem. And improvement teams that do not have access to capital usually will stretch their creativity farther than teams that have been allowed to ask for equipment. If you do leave new capital in scope, be prepared to estimate a return on your requested investment (ROI) or, alternately, identify where savings may be found to offset the capital expense.

9. Out of Scope

Clearly state in the value proposition what will not be addressed by the project. Out of scope may include the activities of upstream suppliers and downstream customers of the value stream. Out of scope does not imply that improvement is not needed, just that these areas are not part of this particular project. St. Luke's excluded two groups of treat and release patients—patients with psychiatric diagnoses and sexual assault victims—as out of scope for its project.

10. Value-Stream Map

Include a high-level map of the major processes in the value-stream (you will work on a detailed map in Chapter 3). Since you've not yet begun to map the value stream in detail, this map will describe the general flow of work.

11. Issues and Problems

Capture a representative list of the specific issues and problems that the stakeholders encounter as they work in the value stream as well as the performance problems that affect the organization.

12. Benefits vs. Impacts

What are the benefits expected if the process is improved? What unintended impacts or consequences might emerge? Remember the beneficiaries of the improved value-stream performance include the customer(s), those who work in the value stream, and the organization. Also remember that improvements (e.g., reduced overtime hours) may have negative consequences for some parts of the value stream (e.g., staff members who rely on the income from working overtime). Unless those impacts are addressed up front, your chances for success will be limited.

At this point you have technically finished the scoping process and are ready to begin planning a value-stream-mapping workshop. The remaining items on the value proposition are included to help you think through who needs to participate in the mapping/workshop sessions and determine the workshop logistics.

13. Workshop Participants

The participants should include frontline staff (the people who actually perform the work in the value stream and in the departments or functions that support or are supported by the value stream). Sometimes small changes to existing IT systems can greatly enhance the ability of a team to make quick improvements. For that reason, it may be helpful to have a member of the IT department as part of the team to experiment with small changes. Try to limit the overall group to seven to 12 individuals—this affords representation from all parts of the value stream you want to improve and all roles involved, but is not so many that more assertive members might dominate a large, dispersed group. Once you've identified participants and their availability, set the logistics for the workshop.

14. Leadership Panel

Typically the leadership panel will consist of the managers/leaders who participated in scoping the project. (Their roles were defined in Chapter 1.)

15. Next Steps

Here you determine responsibilities and timelines for inviting the participants, reserving meeting space, and handling the other logistics and communication tasks necessary to prepare for a mapping workshop, typically a three-day event. And if you have data related to the value-stream performance, compile that for the meeting.

16. Goals

Note that the section for "Goals" on the value proposition has been left blank. Only after identifying problems with the current value stream or processes scoped for the project and developing a future-state value-stream map will you begin to establish goals.

Ground Rules

Most organizations find it helpful to establish ground rules as they plan their projects. Ground rules help define how an improvement team performs and works together. They fall into two categories: how you go about solving the problems (i.e., the methods), and the way you go about working together (i.e., the behavior). Each organization has unique needs and a unique culture. Make sure that you are taking the time to establish the appropriate ground rules so that your efforts will be successful.

Remember, your improvement projects are intended to help your organization solve specific problems in selected value streams and to help those participating learn to work together to make improvements. A few basic "rules of engagement" or "codes of conduct," such as the following, can help.

Codes of Conduct

Method ground rules	Behavioral ground rules
• Only what is in your control (you cannot tell people outside the value stream what to do) • No new capital (or minimal capital investments) • No new full-time-equivalents (FTEs)	• One conversation at a time • Everyone has a chance to participate • No ideas are dumb • Use a "parking lot" for good suggestions that are either out of scope or part of a later phase • Decisions made by consensus, using "agree to proceed"

The Elevator Speech—Communicating Your Intent

For those doing the value-stream improvement work to be truly engaged in the effort, they need to understand why improving the value stream is important. They also should have (and feel that they have) the freedom to propose their own countermeasures to the value-stream problem, even if they differ from leadership's ideas. If team members feel pressured to implement someone else's solution, they will reluctantly take ownership (if at all), and improvements are not likely to get implemented or will not be sustained. Also, if team members don't see the connection to the organizational need, such as strategic quality or cost issues, it will be difficult for them to reach consensus on a future-state design. Without a meaningful, clearly stated purpose, you cannot keep the team focused on developing and implementing specific countermeasures.

A socialization tool that communicates purpose and builds support for the project is an "elevator speech," so-called because it incorporates the amount of information you can deliver in the time it takes an elevator to move between floors—approximately 90 seconds and 250 words. A brief and concise elevator speech also enables listeners to grasp and retell key messages accurately to colleagues (see *St. Luke's Elevator Speech* below).

It is the job of the value-stream owner, lean champion, and lean facilitator to ensure an elevator speech gets developed. The scoping group should write the draft elevator speech, and the rest of improvement team will review the draft and help deliver the final product.

Most elevator speeches include:

• A brief description of the effort,

• What you hope to accomplish,

• Why you want to do it,

• What support you want/need.

St. Luke's Elevator Speech

We've been concerned about our emergency care for a long time, not from a clinical perspective but because of inconsistent and delayed patient flow and incomplete and missing paperwork. In the past it's been difficult for us to sustain many of our improvement efforts, in the ED or elsewhere, but we are going to try a new way. This way—value-stream improvement—will involve all of us working as a team to identify what is really causing problems, redesign our work to eliminate the problems that create constant headaches and workarounds for patients and staff, and, along the way, we will learn new problem-solving skills that will help us to identify and address future problems—or prevent them from occurring in the first place. We need your help in this effort, and ask for your engagement and support.

Chapter 3
Value-Stream Mapping—Current State

This chapter will help you and your team:

• Understand the principles behind mapping.

• Complete a current-state value-stream map for the area
identified in your value proposition.

• Socialize your current-state map with those not on the team
—people who affect, work in, or are affected by the value stream.

• Identify problems by looking for waste in the value stream
(conduct a "waste walk").

• Search out problems that prevent value, flow, work, and
management and learning.

• Gather thoughts about improvements you may consider for
the future state.

Chapter 3
Value-Stream Mapping—Current State

What Is a Value-Stream Map?

Now that you have translated the problem you selected into a manageable scope, it is time to create a value-stream map of your current situation. We use the terms "current state" to refer to the way things work today (the current situation) and "future state" to the way you would like things to work—your vision for the *near-term* future (i.e., one to two years from now). A value-stream map visually represents the flow of work and information that link a product or service to a customer (see *St. Luke's—Current-State Value-Stream Map* for its ED treat-and-release value stream on pages 34–35).

Developing a current-state map creates a common understanding of how things *really work* today in the value stream (not necessarily what the documentation says or some might believe) so that the stakeholders can work together to identify and address problems and make improvements. Remember, see together, learn together, act together.

Mapping forces participants to discuss how they see the value stream. It also forces them to reach consensus on how to represent their perspectives on the map. The map becomes an alignment tool, getting all the participants to talk about the process, not each other. The dialogue becomes, "What's happening?" and "How do you see it?" as opposed to "This is not working ..." and "You should do ..." The map should be a recognition of how much opportunity there is for making improvements.

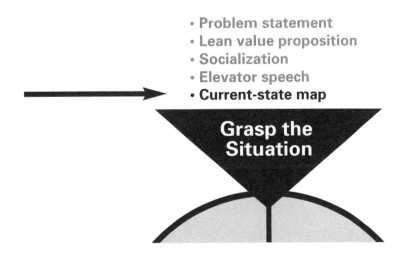

- Problem statement
- Lean value proposition
- Socialization
- Elevator speech
- **Current-state map**

Grasp the Situation

St. Luke's—Current-State Value-Stream Map

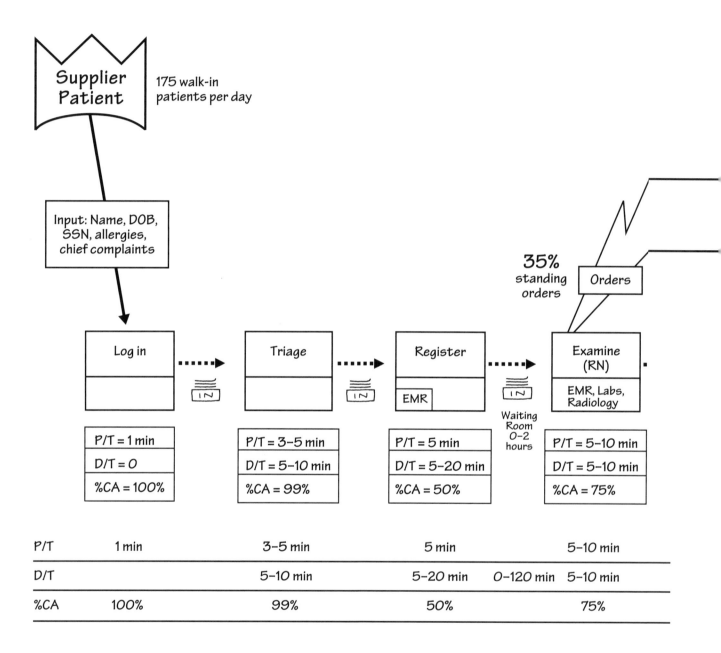

P/T	1 min	3–5 min	5 min		5–10 min
D/T		5–10 min	5–20 min	0–120 min	5–10 min
%CA	100%	99%	50%		75%

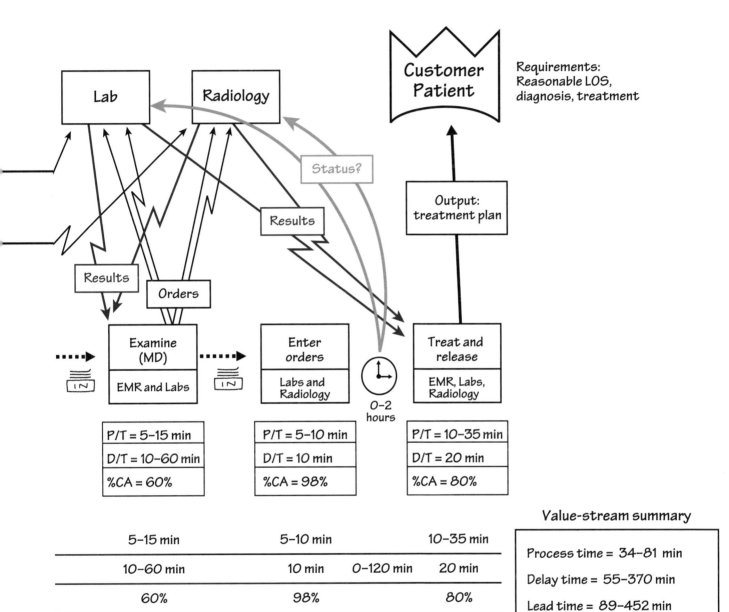

	Lab		Radiology		Customer Patient	

Requirements:
Reasonable LOS,
diagnosis, treatment

Status?

Results

Output:
treatment plan

Results

Orders

Examine (MD)		Enter orders		0–2 hours	Treat and release
EMR and Labs		Labs and Radiology			EMR, Labs, Radiology
P/T = 5–15 min		P/T = 5–10 min			P/T = 10–35 min
D/T = 10–60 min		D/T = 10 min			D/T = 20 min
%CA = 60%		%CA = 98%			%CA = 80%

5–15 min	5–10 min		10–35 min
10–60 min	10 min	0–120 min	20 min
60%	98%		80%

Value-stream summary

Process time = 34–81 min

Delay time = 55–370 min

Lead time = 89–452 min

% Complete and accurate = 17%

PDCA and Mapping

Drawing a current-state value-stream map concludes "grasping the situation" as you work through PDCA. You do not have a complete grasp of the current situation until you have completed a value-stream map. The map and the problems you identify on it complete your definition of the problem, and, at that point, the continuous cycle of PDCA begins and your work transitions to the "plan" of PDCA.

Your first future-state map will be the plan you implement by running experiments. You will check the results of these experiments against your plan (and original problem statement). If the results are what you expect, you will incorporate the changes you have trialed along with clearly defined standards into the normal work of the value stream. If the results of that work are not meeting targets, you will evaluate and analyze, determine new countermeasures (changes you plan to trial to address an identified problem) and plan new experiments. The cycle then becomes continuous.

Keep in mind that PDCA occurs on different levels. For any value-stream improvement project, there are formal PDCA cycles between your future-state mapping and each of the formal reviews that follow, typically at 30-day intervals, until the project ends. Your future state becomes your new current state, which you will revise to become your next future state, and so on.

Whether you will need to conduct a mapping workshop again after reaching your new current state depends on how much change you expect to make in your next cycle. If you are not making major changes to the value stream (e.g., removing entire processes) or revising flow, you will simply update your future-state metrics to drive the next cycle of incremental continuous improvement. However, if you need to do a major redesign of the entire value stream or significant segments of it, you may need to draw a new future-state map. In both cases, you are still following PDCA.

Creating a Value-Stream Map

All value-stream maps are laid out in a horizontal format. They capture major categories or zones of fact finding, each of which will be explained later in this chapter. We find it helpful to think about value-stream maps in terms of the following six zones.

1. The customer is identified in the upper-right corner. The customer is the recipient of the output or outcome of the value-stream. The customer defines the value delivered by the value stream.

2. The supplier is identified in the upper-left corner. The supplier triggers the start of the process. (Note: If the customer also is the supplier—as is the case in St. Luke's map—you also could draw the map with the supplier and customer shown in the same location using just one icon.)

3. The processes in the value stream (process boxes) are located across the middle of the map. A process is a group of activities that together deliver a work product or result that is handed off to the next process.

4. Information flow appears in the upper-middle portion of the map. This area is used to indicate examples of the types of communication with units, departments, or functions outside the value stream that are necessary to make the work progress, including normal communication and efforts to address problems in the functioning of the value stream. A straight arrow represents manual information flow, and a jagged arrow is electronic information flow.

5. Process data or metrics for each process are shown below the processes—each process box has its own data box.

6. A timeline and summary appear at the bottom of the map (see *Value-Stream Metrics* on page 38 for more information).

Working within the six zones, follow these fundamental steps to map your value stream:

1. Customer

On the right side of your map, draw and identify the customer(s) of the process along with the process output(s). Make sure you briefly describe the customer requirements for the process and note those on the map. Initially requirements may include items like "seen in a reasonable time," "length of stay two hours or less," "questions clearly answered," and "appropriate discharge plan." (Quantifiable items are desirable.)

Value-Stream Metrics

As you develop your current-state map, you may want to include data specific to your current state, as well as data specific to the problems you intend to address with your future state.

Recommended value-stream metrics include:

- *Process or processing time (P/T)*: The actual time required to complete the work, sometimes called "hands on time."

- *Delay time (D/T)*: The time the process is delayed. Queues or inboxes represent delays. There can also be delays related to work cycles or for information requests. Document any place where work is typically delayed.

- *Leadtime (L/T)*: Leadtime is the summary metric used to express the total time for a particular process. Leadtime is simply the sum of the processing time and all of the delay time (processing time + delay time = leadtime).

- *Percent complete and accurate (%CA)*: The percentage of the time that all the inputs to the process are complete and accurate when the work in the process box begins. In other words, %CA is the percentage of time that the people performing the work in a particular process have everything they need when and how they need it to begin the work of the process.

Optional metrics:

- *Rework/iterations*: The number of times a particular process is repeated. Iterations can be planned or unplanned, typically representing rework. Note differences between planned and unplanned iterations, and note rework percentages when necessary to illustrate the volume of rework required to complete a process.

- *Number of people/FTEs*: The total number of people or full-time equivalents (FTEs) involved in doing the work. Some processes are performed by many individuals in parallel. You can represent the total staffing with this metric.

- *Total work time*: The total of all the processing time by all the people who are involved with the work. This metric captures the total amount of work time from all participants in a given period. It is nothing more than the sum of all the touch times of all the people involved for all work for all customers. It is usually expressed in terms of your typical timeframe (e.g., one month, one week, etc.).

- *Sentinel events*: In clinical value streams where safety for patients and staff is of particular concern, you may want to capture the number of sentinel events that occur in the value stream.

- *Other*: Your team also may choose to track other data to help tell the story of how well your value stream works today.

2. Supplier

On the left side of your map, draw and identify the supplier(s) of the process and describe the inputs—for example, "number of patients seen in ED per shift or per day."

3. Processes

Draw the basic processes in chronological sequence from left to right, using process boxes to indicate each process in the flow of work. Imagine walking through the value stream, noting each process in sequence. Start by listing the processes before you start to draw the process boxes. This way, you can identify how many process boxes you need and determine where you need to go to gather information.

For each process, draw a process box, label the activity performed during the process, and how the output of the process is delivered to the next process. This will include specific icons for delivery format—electronically, verbally, or in paper form—if the output is information. Work flow is represented with a broken line.

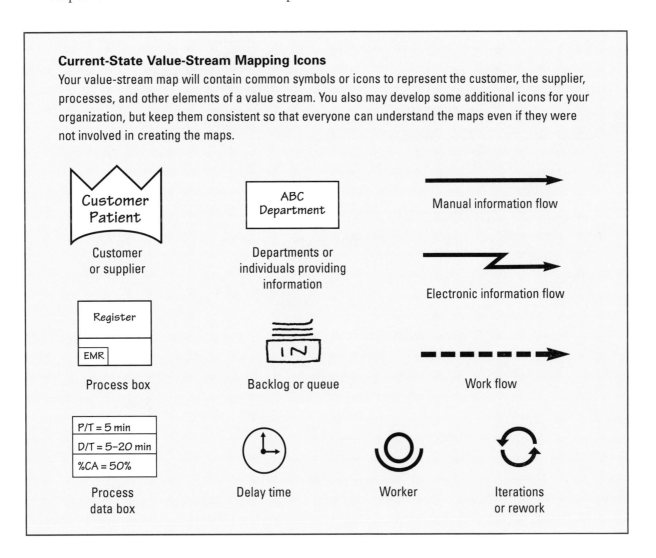

Current-State Value-Stream Mapping Icons

Your value-stream map will contain common symbols or icons to represent the customer, the supplier, processes, and other elements of a value stream. You also may develop some additional icons for your organization, but keep them consistent so that everyone can understand the maps even if they were not involved in creating the maps.

2. Supplier

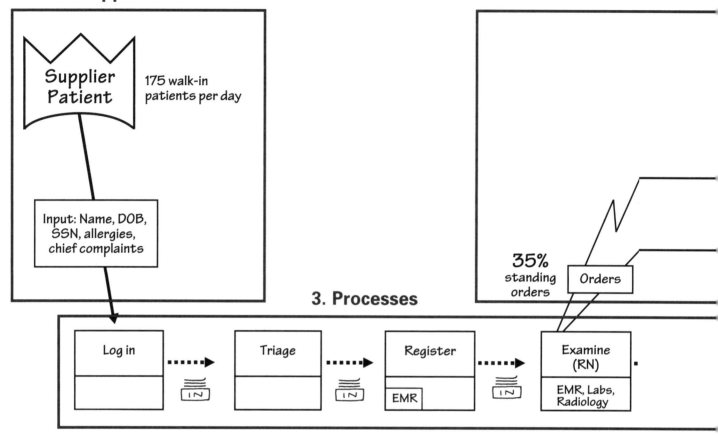

Supplier Patient — 175 walk-in patients per day

Input: Name, DOB, SSN, allergies, chief complaints

35% standing orders — Orders

3. Processes

Log in		Triage		Register		Examine (RN)
				EMR		EMR, Labs, Radiology

IN — IN — IN

4. Information and Communication Flow

You should also identify any communication of information from the process to resources (people or functional areas) outside the process. This communication can occur with the customer(s), supplier(s), other stakeholders, management, or data sources. For example, in the St. Luke's ED, the examination RN communicates the order to Lab and Radiology.

Capturing the communication flow is essential for understanding the entire system because it often determines how well the work flows. As you discover communication with parties or IT systems other than those of the customers/suppliers, draw the recipients of that communication as simple boxes above the process boxes and the specific type of communication to them as arrows. Label each communication line by type (e.g., "request for lab results" or "confirmation of patient identity") so that others can easily understand what occurs.

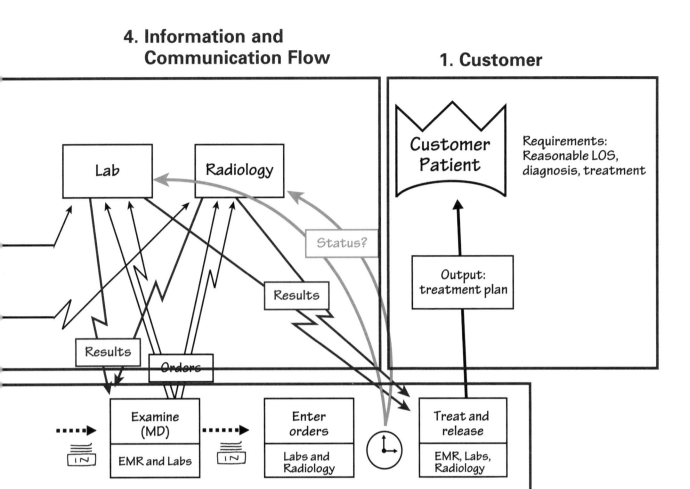

4. Information and Communication Flow

1. Customer

You may find that your map gets messy quickly as you add the communication. Don't worry. Most current-state maps have messy communication, but it all needs to be included to document what it takes to make the work progress.

You may need to experiment a little to find the right "altitude" for your map. Current-state maps generally have between five and 15 process boxes on them (St. Luke's treat and release ED map has seven process boxes). With too few boxes, it can be difficult to see the systemic problems, especially all the rework and communication outside the process that may be contributing to or causing waste. If there are too many process boxes, the map becomes so complex that barriers to flow and other problems get obscured by all the detail. In general, if you have scoped your project to a small segment of a value stream (such as the discharge process of an ED value stream), you will probably have a small number of process boxes (five to seven). Alternately, if you have defined a scope that starts with a patient arrival and ends with discharge, your map may have 20 or more process boxes.

When identifying the processes along your value stream, you may encounter a flow that merges or divides. For example in the ED, one patient may need lab tests and a CT scan. Drawing blood and the patient's visit to Radiology might be sequential process boxes, but the results will be processed in parallel. Once *both* sets of results are complete, a provider can then determine a diagnosis, or order more tests. You would draw these flows above one another when the activities are truly parallel and independent, like the radiologist reading films and the lab analyzing the blood sample (see *Process Flows Merging, Dividing* below). Don't try to draw every flow if there are too many; choose the primary flows first and, if necessary, rescope others later as separate improvement efforts.

5. Process metrics

Beneath each process box identify data for the process. For your current-state map, you can use ranges and/or averages for the data. Ranges can be especially revealing when you look for improvement opportunities later.

Unlike work environments containing physical products and precise amounts of inventory that are known and regularly tracked (e.g., manufacturing), using ranges and/or averages is frequently necessary in hospital settings because the people doing the mapping do not always have the luxury of observing and measuring the work directly. An example of a range is the 5 to 20 minutes of delay time in registration on the St. Luke's map.

Process Flows Merging, Dividing

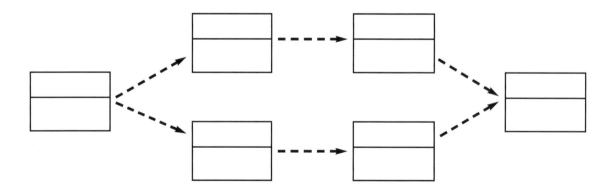

Ranges also capture the variation of a particular process—for example, the differences in leadtime among shifts in the ED. For these reasons, ranges that are directionally accurate (but not exact) are typically precise enough to enable you to grasp the current situation. Moreover, when there is variation, the ranges may sometime tell a more complete story. Whether you are using single figures or ranges, select numbers that capture what happens most of the time (e.g., ~80%) and don't worry about the "outliers" for now. Otherwise, you'll end up revising your process based on things that rarely happen rather than what typically occurs.

As you move through the value stream, document the delays with a delay icon, both between the processes, as well as within each process box. Some of these delays will be caused by a queue or a backlog, where downstream resources do not have enough capacity to handle all the work. As a result, work piles up. These queues can be anything you can count (e.g., patients, forms, requests, etc.). Indicate the queues with an in-box icon. Other delays are not caused by queues but by resources or information not being available, such as when surgical instruments are missing from the kits supplied for a given procedure.

We represent these pure delays with a clock icon. On the St. Luke's map, there is a pure delay just prior to the treat-and-release process (see below).

5. Process metrics

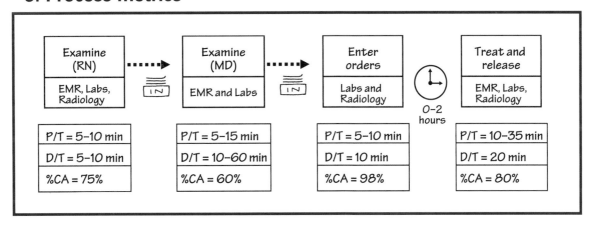

6. Timeline and summary with value-stream metrics

To complete your map, draw a timeline and/or summary box. If you used ranges when applying metrics to the process boxes, make sure you sum both the lowest and highest figures to arrive at your process time (P/T) and delay time (D/T) totals.

To get the total percentage complete and accurate (%CA) for your value stream, convert the score for each process box into a decimal and multiply them all together, then convert them back into a percentage. Similarly, if you used ranges for %CA, calculate your lowest and highest range. This will give you an estimate of the probability that each piece of work (or each patient) can go through the entire value stream without encountering any problems (e.g., delays, rework, or workarounds). When you have a value stream with parallel flows, apply data for the primary flow (that which consumes the most leadtime).

Additional Information

You should title and date your map as well as include a version number. As you socialize the map with others who work in the value stream, some findings will change. Version labeling will help to keep everyone working with the most current version of the map.

As you construct your map, stay focused on the "as-is." Most groups tend to jump to solutions when creating a value-stream map. Remember, before the map is complete (and socialized), you don't yet completely understand the current situation. When you allow discussions to drift to "solutions" it has the effect of shutting people off and can result in actions that do not really address the underlying problems. Keep a "parking lot" list to capture possible solutions and questions related to scope. You can always refer to them again when you begin designing the future state.

6. Timeline and summary

P/T	1 min	3–5 min	5 min		5–10 min
D/T		5–10 min	5–20 min	0–120 min	5–10 min
%CA	100%	99%	50%		75%

Mapping Mechanics

There are various ways that your team can physically create its value-stream map. We recommend drawing by hand on a large white-board or drawing on dry-erase presentation sheets. Presentation sheets work well because the dry-erase surface allows for editing during the mapping exercise and because the sheets can be transported to other locations for sharing. Some people prefer to map using large sticky notes with lines that represent process data boxes. Using the sticky notes on dry-erase sheets allows you to shift the content and sequence of the processes easily. Be aware that sticky notes may come off the map as you transport it to different locations.

There are two other methods you might consider to transport your map: digital photos or a smaller, transcribed version. Take a digital photo of the large map, and then print and distribute smaller versions that can be marked with changes and comments. You also can present digital photos as slides and solicit feedback from a group. Alternately, you can transcribe a smaller version of your maps on 11 x 17 inch paper and use small sticky notes for the process boxes. This format also can be used by participants to make changes and give feedback.

Do not get frustrated if your maps get messy. It means you've done a good job of capturing the chaos in the way the value stream currently works, which will soon present opportunities for making it work better.

5–15 min	5–10 min		10–35 min	Value-stream summary
10–60 min	10 min	0–120 min	20 min	Process time = 34–81 min
60%	98%		80%	Delay time = 55–370 min
				Lead time = 89–452 min
				% Complete and accurate = 17%

Socializing Your Value-Stream Map

A value-stream map should represent an agreement on how things work today. For that reason, the current-state map must include input from everyone who performs work in the value stream. When the mapping is done in a workshop, the team will take the draft back to socialize it and gain consensus. Because others who will see the map do not have the same background in mapping, you will need to provide them with an overview of mapping and have your value proposition available to keep the dialogue focused.

Keep in mind that up until this point, all the items you have socialized (your problem statement, value proposition and elevator speech) have not involved new tools, just new formats. For that reason, it can be helpful to show those outside the improvement team an example that is not their value stream (such as the one in this guide), and explain the meaning of the icons, zones, and metrics you are using. Be as descriptive as necessary, such as discussing the different types of delays (between-process delays vs. internal delays).

System-Level Problems

As you socialize the map, people will begin to see the value stream in its entirety, often for the first time. At this point, some on your team may be confident that you have accurately documented how the value stream works, but others may feel (with justification) that the map fails to tell the complete story.

To capture the "rest of the story," you need to document problems in the value stream on your current-state map. Remember that in healthcare most value streams and processes were not designed: they evolved over time, driven by individual and departmental needs, often at the expense of the output of the larger system.

Formally documenting the problems will help complete your understanding of the current state. To do this you will identify and document:

• Eight forms of waste in the value stream and

• Value, flow, work, and management and learning in the value stream (or lack thereof).

Developing Eyes for Waste

In healthcare organizations, most people associate waste with out-of-date or contaminated materials and supplies and biological specimens that need to be discarded. In lean organizations, however, people recognize that there are many other types of waste that impact the quality and efficiency of value streams and, for that reason, it's important to learn how to recognize them.

Learning to recognize waste (a process symptom) as a way to identify problems in a value stream is analogous to learning to differentiate pain (a patient symptom) in order to help determine what steps are needed to reach a diagnosis. Knowing that a patient is experiencing pain and that he or she has a pain score of 7 is useful information. However, knowing precisely where in the body the pain is occurring and what was happening when the pain began—localized or radiating, sharp or dull, constant or intermittent, is or is not relieved by changing position or some other action—provides a much better basis for selecting next steps in reaching a diagnosis. Similarly, knowing what kind of waste is occurring and where within the process of a value stream provides important information about problems. Waste is never a problem in and of itself. Rather, like pain, it is a symptom of one or more underlying problems in the system.

The initial seven forms of waste originated from the Toyota Production System. They describe waste at a process level, where the actual work is being performed. More recently, lean practitioners have added an eighth type of waste—the waste of people's knowledge, skills, and abilities. Each type of waste (see *DOWNTIME of Waste* on page 48) has an equivalent in healthcare settings.

It is a maxim in lean thinking that to fix any problem you must first see the waste. However, the longer you have worked in a system, the harder it is to see the waste around you. Taking a "waste walk" is one way to make the waste visible again. A waste walk is simply a planned visit to where work is being performed to observe what's happening and to note the waste. It differs from go-see activities in that you are specifically looking for waste.

Common objectives for your waste walks include:

• Validate the problems pointed out in the development of the current-state map.

• Provide a format to continue to socialize the redesign effort.

• Provide an initial opportunity to gather staff ideas about the current-state problems.

DOWNTIME of Waste

Waste	Examples
D = Defects producing and correcting	• Missing or incomplete information, equipment missing, medication errors, wrong patient, wrong procedure, blood redraws, misdirected results, wrong bills • Rework of any process • Injuries to patients or staff
O = Overproduction and production of unwanted products	• Syringes filled with flu vaccines – before required • Testing and treatment done ahead of time to suit staff schedules and equipment use, medication given early • Many types of documentation
W = Waiting idle time of patient or staff	• Patient waiting for prescriptions, checkout, appointment, or bed • Waiting for test results, records, information, equipment • Staff waiting for meds, blood draw, transport, OR cleaning • ED staff waiting for admission, can't see next patient
N = Not utilizing the knowledge, skills and abilities of all employees	• Unwillingness to consider an idea and experiment with that idea • Limiting the opportunity for all people to be problem solvers
T = Transport relocating patients, equipment, and supplies	• Moving radiology reports, specimens, meds • Moving of patients from floor to floor for testing
I = Inventory excess equipment, supplies, waiting patients	• Supplies, pharmacy stock, test kits, lab supplies, specimens awaiting analysis, bed assignments • Expired supplies that must be disposed of yet still stocked
M = Motion movement by workers	• Searching for charts, supplies, paperwork, patients, meds • Layout causing unnecessary walking, long clinic halls • Leaving exam room for prescriptions, patient education materials
E = Extra processing unnecessary steps, questions, paperwork	• Time/date stamps on forms but never used • Multiple consent forms and other repeated paperwork • Retesting and repeat registration • Charge tickets • Bed moves

The following material will be beneficial to you and your implementation team (including team representatives of the different functions) as you conduct your waste walk:

• Copies of your current-state map (including problems already identified),

• Examples of the various wastes,

• A standard template for team members to record observations from the waste walk (see *Waste Walk Sheet* on page 50 or download a copy at *lean.org/ppj*),

• Your lean facilitator walking with your team, especially if most members are conducting their first waste walk.

Now you're ready to begin your waste walk! We suggest the following approach.

Waste Walk Guidelines

1. Huddle with your team members:
   - Describe the purpose,
   - Describe the various forms of wastes and examples,
   - Pass out copies of the current-state map and identified problems, and
   - Assign areas to walk to you team. It's usually better to have a pair of people for each assignment.

2. As a group walk the whole value stream depicted on your map to confirm the areas of the individual/pair assignments.

3. Explain to the people in the area of observation what you are doing. Share the map and waste examples and describe the objectives of the observation activity.

4. Move to areas for individual assignments, and study the areas for 30–45 minutes.

5. As you see work that appears to be waste, jot down the example you see.

6. Return to the team and discuss what you have seen.

7. As a team, match the wastes you see to problems previously identified in the current-state map. If other significant problems are identified during the walk, place them on the map.

8. Put the results of the waste walk next to the current-state map being shared in the area and use the examples to continue to socialize the current state and the system-level problems that frustrate the people and process.

Waste Walk Sheet

Waste Category	Observation	Impact on value-stream performance	Value-stream "problem type" (customer, flow, work, learning, management)	Possible solutions from people doing the work
Defects producing and correcting				
Overproduction and production of unwanted products				
Waiting idle time of patient or staff				
Not utilizing the knowledge, skills and abilities of all employees				
Transportation relocating patients, equipment, and supplies				
Inventory excess equipment, supplies, waiting patients				
Motion movement by workers				
Extra processing unnecessary steps, questions, paperwork				

A blank waste walk template and other resources are available at *lean.org/ppj*

Waste Walk Helpful Hints

- It's better to walk an area you *may not* be familiar with as "new eyes are good eyes" to the normal work patterns.

- Current-state problems can be a combination of several wastes. Always keep an open mind.

- Many examples of waste you see can have more than one category: don't get hung up on agreeing on exactly which category the waste is.

- Be sure you are seeing all the work associated with your area. Don't be afraid to move around within the area.

- Feel free to talk to the people doing the work. They may be frustrated about what they see and have some thoughts on improvements. But listen to their suggestions for improvement with an open mind as they may not have a "system" perspective as opposed to a "personal" perspective on the improvement. Put their suggestions down in the column marked "possible solutions from those doing the work."

- Be respectful of those you encounter and the work they are doing.

Developing Eyes for Value, Flow, Work, and Management and Learning

Now that you have looked at symptoms occurring with the work and identified wastes, you and your team are ready to refocus on the actual problems. Lean looks at those problems from the perspectives of value, flow, work, and management and learning. These four categories will be explained in more detail in Chapter 4, but it is important to begin thinking about them now. They relate to your current state because they form the basis for creating a lean value stream.

Value refers to the value of the output to the end customer and to the customer for each process inside the value stream. A key principle here is that the customer defines value, not the people producing the output. *Flow* refers to the extent to which work progresses smoothly through the processes and through the value stream. Like fever and pain when diagnosing a patient, flow is a key diagnostic sign of how a value stream functions. When work is not flowing smoothly, it usually signals a broken process, one that involves lots of delays, defects, and rework that create no value and add huge costs.

Work refers to the way in which the work is performed inside each process—does it produce quality outputs that are free from defects (i.e., outputs that address patients' needs and that are safe for patients and staff)? *Managing and learning* means that the value stream is designed in such a way that the people working in the processes can identify problems quickly and respond to them in a way that gets things back on track. It also means that as problems are addressed, whatever is learned gets shared and fed back into the system so that the same problems are not repeated.

Below are ways to recognize problems in these four categories. Use the questions to uncover underlying problems in your system, and be aware that many problems can fall into more than one category.

Value

Look at the output of the value stream and compare it to the customer requirements. How well is the value stream meeting those requirements? Determine if there are any gaps between the actual value-stream outcomes and what the customer(s) really needs:

- Overproduction (giving the customer something he/she is not willing to pay for or does not need),
- Not delivering the product or service the customer really wants,
- Not meeting needs for delivery frequency and/or timing,
- Not meeting quality expectations.

Flow

Problems in flow are exemplified by unnecessary delays. How well is the work progressing from one process to the next? Does one process start too early (without good information) just to get a head start? Or does work start too late because there is no clear trigger? Are there fluctuations in workload (e.g., periods of coasting along followed by a flurry of activity and firefighting)? On the map, symptoms of breakdowns in flow will be visible between processes and in how work is triggered:

- Waiting/delay,
- Rework,
- Excessive handoffs,
- Interruptions,
- Many requirements for decisions and approvals,
- Poorly defined requirements,
- Different work for a common process,
- Expectations too high.

Work

Look at the actual work within the processes as well as steps within each process. Determine if quality is built into the activity. Symptoms of problems within processes are often related to standards. Is there rework because a previous process was not complete or accurate or because there are no clear standards for the work? Are there quality problems because there is no standardized (best practice) way to perform a task that should be standardized? Is there evidence of *ad hoc* workarounds that have gradually become part of the normal process that now require additional resources?

On the map, look at the processes and their data boxes to determine problems in doing the work, such as:

- Rework,
- Passing work without checking for completeness and accuracy,
- Standards not being followed (workarounds) or no standards.

Management and learning

To properly manage a value stream you have to know what is happening within it. Is the status of each part of the value stream visible? Are there mechanisms to readily identify problems of value, flow, and work? How effective is the value stream serving the customer? How well is work flowing? How efficient are the resources being used? Are there any quality issues? Is the sole focus (if any) on end results instead of including in-process measures that can help drive real-time countermeasures and improvement?

When looking for management problems, you are really determining if improving and learning are integrated into the value stream and the work. Are you encountering the same problems over and over without really solving them? Does the value stream have points where someone is checking to see that everything upstream is working the way it should and producing what is required by the value stream? Is improvement viewed in terms of an event or intervention instead of the way work is performed and managed on an ongoing basis? In other words, are lean changes regularly made with the scientific method (PDCA) and incorporated within daily work activities?

It is difficult to pinpoint management and learning problems directly on your map. They often are systemic to the entire value stream. To explore problems in this category, a brief discussion can help surface the symptoms related to management.

You will want to record management problems on the bottom or top of the map, such as:

- No clearly defined owner for managing the process,
- No reviews,
- No performance metrics (and targets),
- No management corrective-action process until too late,
- Many reviews, but no corrective actions,
- Limited reuse of existing information,
- Learning is not integrated in the process.

Value-Stream Improvement is Lean Management

Do not get discouraged if it seems like there are too many problems to tackle and that your present management system is unable to address them. Recognize that what you are doing is the first step to *lean management*. You are starting to use the scientific method. Your team is grasping the situation and will soon be developing a plan for improvement. The steps you are taking form the foundation of a lean management system that engages staff in problem solving on an ongoing basis.

Pay attention to the methods you are using to socialize the problem-solving tools. Keep up a routine of the methods that work and continue to perform PDCA on those that don't. For example, if having weekly sessions with groups of five to seven people from a single function promotes healthy dialogue, then plan to continue using that method. If you try cross-functional groups and get no feedback, then perhaps keeping people functionally segmented is necessary (for now). You can decide if promoting cross-functional communication is a problem you want to solve now or put in your parking lot. Remember, you can use PDCA on the methods you use to solve problems as well as the particular problems you are solving.

St. Luke's Current-State Map

St. Luke's team identified the ED treat-and-release value stream for improvement. This consists of processes for walk-in patients, which begin as they enter the ED door. After reading a multitude of signs, walk-ins find their way to a desk next to security staff, who direct them to:

1. **Log in** at the preregistration desk. They are then directed to the triage nurse. If the nurse is with another patient there are three available chairs where the patient waits.

2. **Triage** of the patient occurs once the triage nurse is free.

3. **Registration** is the next process step for the patient. Necessary information is missing much of the time, but the paperwork is filled out as much as possible, entered into the EMR system, and the patient is asked to wait. When a room is free the patient is directed to a room.

4. An **RN exam** is performed by a nurse, who documents it in the EMR. There is typically some missing information (Rx lists, patient history). Labs occasionally are ordered from standing order protocols using the software system, but the nurses sometimes get into trouble with a few of the doctors who believe that they should see the patient first before any labs are ordered. The patient then waits for the physician in the exam room.

5. An **MD exam** is begun by a physician. This usually involves reassessing the patient as the nursing notes frequently are too time-consuming to find in the EMR. Other information is sometimes missing from earlier handoffs. The exam is then completed and documented in the EMR with orders left to be processed.

6. The nurse **enters orders** for the patient using either software for Labs or software for Radiology. The nurse also fills out one of five possible Lab forms to manually document the lab requests. The patient then waits for the results. When the physician has time, he/she will check for results and may call to expedite the results.

7. When the results arrive, the patient is then **treated and released** by the physician. This often can take a while as the paperwork is missing some documentation and signatures, and the discharge nurse is responsible for searching for the nurse/physician to complete the data. Both the EMR and the other paperwork are completed.

Based on performances for the ED value stream and observations of it including a waste walk, St. Luke's team developed a current-state value-stream map, noting four significant problems:

    1. Long patient delays in the waiting area,

    2. Standing work orders used only 35% of the time,

    3. Excess wait time for Lab and Radiology,

    4. Quality issues with discharge instructions.

See *St. Luke's Current-State Value-Stream Map—Problems Identified* on pages 56–57.

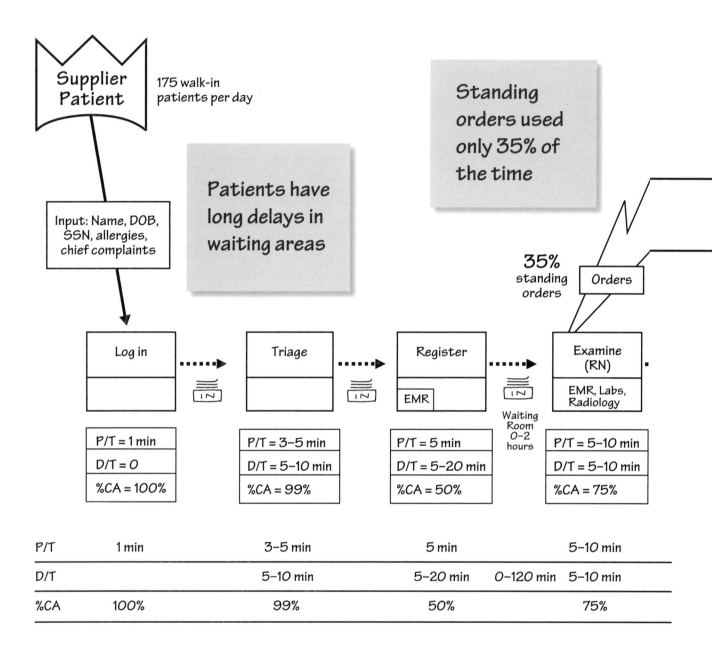

P/T	1 min	3-5 min	5 min		5-10 min
D/T		5-10 min	5-20 min	0-120 min	5-10 min
%CA	100%	99%	50%		75%

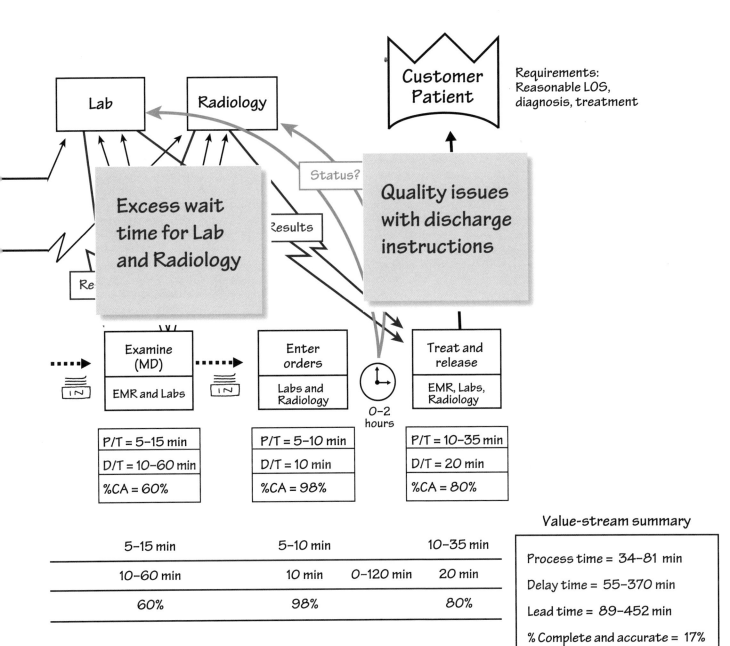

Lab

Radiology

Customer Patient

Requirements: Reasonable LOS, diagnosis, treatment

Excess wait time for Lab and Radiology

Status?

Results

Quality issues with discharge instructions

Re...

Examine (MD)		Enter orders		Treat and release
EMR and Labs		Labs and Radiology	0-2 hours	EMR, Labs, Radiology

P/T = 5–15 min	P/T = 5–10 min	P/T = 10–35 min
D/T = 10–60 min	D/T = 10 min	D/T = 20 min
%CA = 60%	%CA = 98%	%CA = 80%

5–15 min	5–10 min		10–35 min
10–60 min	10 min	0–120 min	20 min
60%	98%		80%

Value-stream summary

Process time = 34–81 min

Delay time = 55–370 min

Lead time = 89–452 min

% Complete and accurate = 17%

Chapter 4
Future-State Mapping

This chapter will help you and your team:

• Grasp the characteristics of lean value streams.

• Learn guidelines to develop a future-state map.

• Translate guidelines into key questions to analyze and define the future-state map.

• Socialize your future-state vision and present to leadership.

Chapter 4
Future-State Mapping

Designing a Lean Value Stream

Once you have a socialized your *current-state map*, complete with the problem descriptions resulting from your waste walks and subsequent discussions, it's time to create a vision of how you want things to work. Just as you and your team needed a common understanding of the problem (and the reason for solving it) in order to work together to address it, so, too, must you have a common vision of where you want to go.

You probably have already received several opinions on how to fix the problem. It's important to resist the temptation to jump to those solutions without going through the process of developing and agreeing on a future-state map. Jumping in too quickly without taking time to develop a common vision for how the value stream should function can result in confusion, false starts, or even results that degrade performance instead of improve it.

The *future-state map* provides a mechanism by which all the stakeholders can reach agreement on a future-state vision. It is the first phase in establishing a "plan" for the improvements needed to realize the vision.

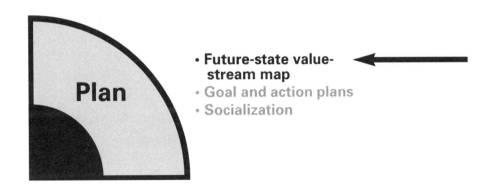

Plan

- **Future-state value-stream map** ⟵
- Goal and action plans
- Socialization

What Makes a Value Stream Lean?

Before you address the problems in your value stream to make it more lean, you'll find it helpful to have a clear picture of what a truly lean value stream looks like. A lean value stream exhibits the following characteristics:

1. The value stream produces precisely what the end customer requires (*value*), and each process in the value stream produces what the next process requires exactly when it is needed, how it is needed, and how much is needed.

2. The work *flows* smoothly through the value stream with no waiting or rework and with the information necessary to perform the work available when it is needed.

3. *Work* is standardized so that each step uses the best current method and the best sequence for the process, problems are surfaced quickly and addressed appropriately, and quality of work is confirmed as work occurs.

4. Regular milestones are established to monitor and evaluate how well the value stream is working, and lessons learned are fed back into the process and into the organization as a whole (i.e., the process itself is *managed*, not just the people).

Now that you can recognize a lean value stream, it's time to design your own, one that delivers an output that meets customer requirements, involves the least waste (time, money, resources), and provides the medium to establish a foundation for lean management on which continuous value-stream improvement is routine instead of crisis driven.

Your future-state mapping will follow guidelines to establish value, flow, work, and management. Decision-making to define a future state will be spurred by translating the guidelines into questions that you and your team collectively answer. The answers to those questions will help you analyze your options and develop your future-state map.

Step through the following guidelines and questions in order. The remainder of this chapter addresses guidelines to improve value, flow, and work and the techniques to support that work. As you go through the questions, mark your current-state map with your changes in another color that clearly stands out. After answering all the questions and representing your ideas on the map, you will then draw a *clean version* of your proposed future state.

Guidelines and Questions for a Lean Value Stream

	Guidelines	Questions
Value	1. Match value stream output to customer requirements (e.g., timing, quantity, quality).	1. What are the customer requirements for timing, quantity, and quality? What are the requirements for the end customer? What are the requirements for each internal customer (i.e., each chunk)?
Flow	2a. Develop continuous flow wherever possible (including use of service-level agreements). 2b. Define how the progression of work will be signaled where continuous flow is not possible. 2c. Level resource capacity to address changes in work type or volume.	2a. Where can you establish continuous flow? Where can you improve flow using service-level agreements? 2b. How will you signal work to progress where continuous flow is not possible? Where does work get released to the next process? What type of signal will work to signal the upstream process that the next process is ready to receive the work? 2c. How will you level resource capability? Where does the unevenness in work type or volume most often occur? What options can you use to level your resources? Do you need to implement cross-training?
Work	3. Establish stability and confirmation of quality with clearly defined work standards and standardized work.	3. Where will you use work standards and standardized work to establish stability and built-in quality?
Management	4a. Create measures and mechanisms that allow you to see and respond to problems quickly. 4b. Periodically reflect on value stream performance and incorporate lessons learned.	4. How will you manage and continue to improve the value stream? (*Chapters 5–8 provide information about creating metrics and other mechanisms to surface problems and allow quick responses as well as using reflection to promote organizational learning.*)

Your team will focus on the need identified in your problem statement and create a future-state vision that includes *enough change* to have an impact on this issue. You are not trying to solve all the problems in the current state, but instead trying to make significant improvements based on team consensus. By focusing on the value stream, its processes, and the associated behaviors, you can achieve real performance improvement, learn about the approach, and do so in a manageable timeframe (i.e., a series of 90-to-120 day projects).

If you aim too high (or too far into the future), you are liable to be discouraged when the implementation stalls from changes out of your control or just plain fatigue. Keep in mind that you are establishing ongoing ownership and visibility. Just because a problem is not addressed now doesn't mean that it will never be addressed. Changes that may take a longer time to implement can always be included later as you cycle through PDCA or create a new future-state vision down the road.

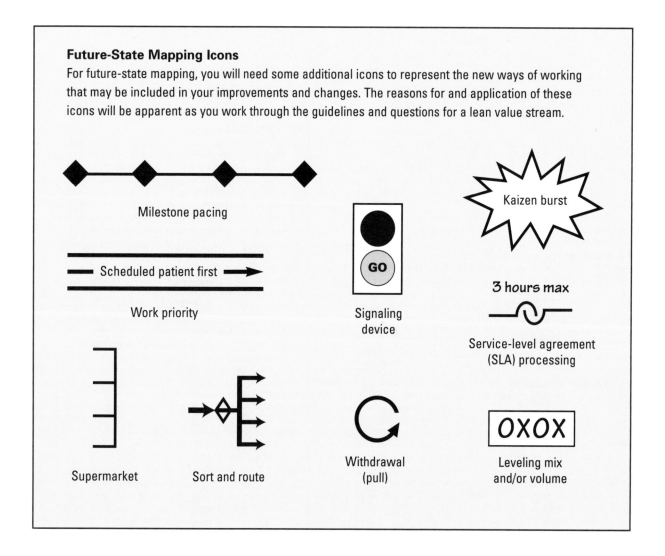

Future-State Mapping Icons

For future-state mapping, you will need some additional icons to represent the new ways of working that may be included in your improvements and changes. The reasons for and application of these icons will be apparent as you work through the guidelines and questions for a lean value stream.

Milestone pacing

Scheduled patient first

Work priority

Signaling device

Kaizen burst

3 hours max

Service-level agreement (SLA) processing

Supermarket

Sort and route

Withdrawal (pull)

OXOX

Leveling mix and/or volume

Your problem statement directs how you will apply changes to improve your value stream. These changes can be applied from two different perspectives, in conjunction or independently:

- To close a gap between the existing output to a customer (current performance) and customer requirements (ideal performance). *Value*, including safety, should always be your initial focus for improvement, ensuring that you will improve (or at least hold constant) the output to the customer.

- To improve the efficiency of the system that provides or delivers the output (i.e., you may currently be giving the customer what they want but you're doing so in an inefficient manner that costs the organization excess time, money, resources, etc.). The remaining three problem categories—*flow*, *work*, and *management*—affect the efficiency of the system in delivering outputs. Holding constant (or improving) the efficiency of the system also will help your organization more clearly focus on *value*.

Value-Stream Improvement—Two Perspectives

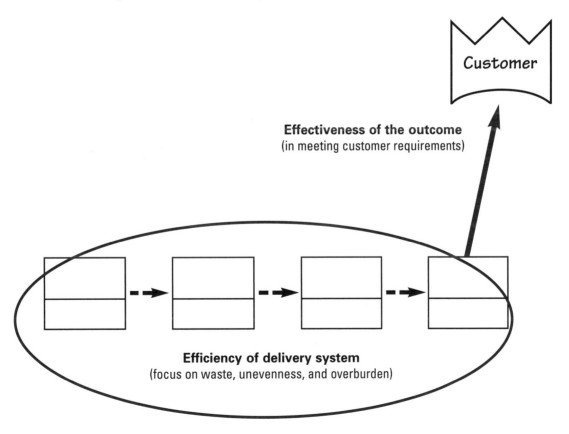

In healthcare settings, these two perspectives are closely linked because patients do not just receive the outcome, they are a part of the process. For example, the time a patient has to wait for a provider and for lab tests to be reviewed both clearly relate to the internal flow of the work (efficiency). However, these situations also relate to patient satisfaction (effectiveness), since patients would prefer to be seen and treated in a timely fashion. For that reason, healthcare value-stream improvement efforts that involve patient care typically focus on both *outcome effectiveness* and *value-stream efficiency*.

Create your vision for the future by starting with the customer to determine if you are meeting customer requirements, and then design a lean value stream in which each process provides only and exactly what the next process needs when it needs it. Link all the processes together in an efficient delivery system where value flows all the way through to the customer in the shortest time, with the highest quality, and at the most appropriate effort.

Guideline 1: Match value-stream output to customer requirements (timing, quality, and quantity).

Improving value-stream performance always starts with the customer. Because most healthcare processes are focused on clinical outcomes defined by providers, rather than being thoughtfully designed to serve all the needs of the customer, you should start with an analysis of what the customer defines as value. Comparing the value-stream output to customer requirements will help highlight the need for specific improvements and build commitment among your team to the overall future-state vision.

Work backward from the customer. Ignore the deliverable output that you and your team have marked on the current-state map. Instead, determine what quality *really means to the customer*. If possible, go directly to your customers. Ask them what they want. If the value stream you have chosen serves external customers (i.e., patients), you may have direct access to a representative sample of customers. (Patient satisfaction survey data may be helpful, but, in many cases, you will need more targeted information than what's found on survey reports. Patient advocacy groups may help supply information.) For value streams serving internal customers (e.g., other units within your facility), get the facts directly. If these internal customers have not been a part of the mapping activity, now is the time to talk to them about their requirements. (For example, Lab and Radiology are both internal customers and suppliers for most clinical value streams. Establishing what they require as customers to be able to turn work around in a required time frame is a good way to establish common expectations about these mutual requirements.)

Consider the method of service delivery as well as the quality. After gaining a better understanding of customers' quality needs (i.e., error-free), find out as much as possible about how the customer values the service component. When does the customer expect the outcome? How often is communication required? How much communication is necessary, and how does the customer want it delivered?

Do you need more insight into the patterns of demand? For example, do you frequently find days or shifts where the department is under/overstaffed with regard to your ability to meet customer demand irrespective of the actual number of personnel on duty? Investigate further to find out what's really going on.

Who Is Your Customer? What Does Your Customer Require?

As you begin designing your future-state vision, it's a good idea to revisit whom you have designated as your customer. If your project scope includes an entire value stream, you may want to separate that stream into smaller groups of processes and flow based on the customers served and what they need. As at St. Luke's Hospital, for example, most EDs include at least one flow for level 1 and 2 patients who will likely be stabilized and admitted or transferred to another facility, another flow for patients who will be treated and discharged, and perhaps additional flows for patients with acute mental-health problems and for victims of sexual assault. The desired LOS and the other customer requirements for each of these value streams may vary significantly.

If you have scoped your project to address one or two segments of your value stream (e.g., door to doc, discharge to transition, doctor's orders to lab results received), remember that, although the end customer for clinical value streams is the patient, the customer for your value-stream segment may be the physicians or some other internal group. Internal customer requirements will be different from, but should complement, those for the patient.

Some of your value-stream requirements may not originate from the actual customer, but may come from other sources. For example, some of the metrics you have been asked to track are based on recommended LOS or other metrics that originate with the Centers for Medicare & Medicaid Service or the Joint Commission. Others, such as total LOS or door-to-doc time for treat-and-release patients, may be dictated by your competition and whatever they are marketing to your community. At some point, however, those times will become your customers' expectations as they compare you to your competitors.

Once you identify what the customer values in terms of quality, timing, and quantity, you can design a value stream that meets the needs of the customer while consuming the appropriate resources. To do that you need to determine the primary *"chunks"* of activity in the value stream. To identify the chunks in a value stream, you zoom out (remember zoom control?) to get a big-picture view, look at the customer requirements, and identify the major activities required to deliver that value. (These activities *are not typically* the individual process boxes that appear on your current-state map, although in some cases a single process box may serve as a "chunk.")

Chunking usually involves grouping several process boxes into recognizable, related activities, e.g., scheduling, invoicing, etc. To identify the chunks in your value stream, look for major transformations in the creation of the product, service, or information produced by the stream. Or look for changes in the nature of the work performed and/or the people or units who perform the work. (See page 69 for how St. Luke's divided its treat-and-release value stream into chunks.)

Identifying chunks helps people who work in the process get a perspective beyond their individual activities or functions and to focus on the entire value-delivery system. When designing the future state, this early focus on larger segments of the system (as opposed to the individual processes) helps avoid suboptimizing (i.e., improving the function of one part of the value stream at the expense of overall value-stream performance or the performance of other parts). It also provides a tool to help the team to reach consensus on the overall direction for the future-state vision. And it helps identify places to measure the quality of handoffs and identify "in-process" metrics to help you assess how the different sections of the value stream are performing.

Chunks in the Value Stream

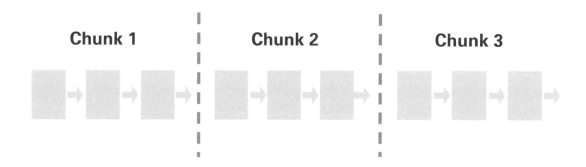

Once you've established the framework for the future state by chunking the value stream, you need to examine each handoff or interface at the boundaries between chunks. Work forward from the supplier, identifying the inputs. The input to the first chunk should be whatever the supplier provides that signals the entire value stream to begin, e.g., a physician writes an order for a patient to be admitted to medical ICU.

As you move from left to right on the map, each interface represents a supplier-customer relationship: The chunk to the left of the interface is the supplier for the customer chunk to the right of the interface. The output of the final chunk (for example, *Chunk 3* in the graphic below) should match the end-customer requirements for quality, timing, and quantity. (*Note*: Some people prefer to chunk backward from end customer to the supplier to ensure that everything leading to the final output is aligned to produce what the end customer requires.)

As you identify each chunk and its output(s), clearly determine who the customer is for the chunk and the customer's requirements. The customer requirements are what that chunk requires (the input) in order to perform the work necessary to provide the next chunk or provide the required output or deliverable to the end customer, e.g., what medical ICU needs from the admitting physician to get the patient into a bed and get treatment initiated. As suppliers and customers engage in a dialogue around inputs and requirements, it quickly becomes apparent that many suppliers have little understanding of what their customers (the downstream chunk) really need.

Interfaces between Chunks

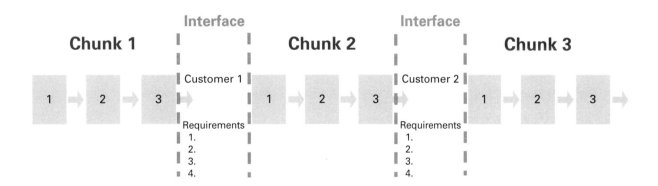

Question 1: What are the (real) customer requirements for timing, quality, and quantity?

Answer this question directly on your map (in a different color), starting with the end customer. Then divide the map into chunks, drawing vertical broken lines at the boundary between each chunk. Determine the overall purpose of each chunk and label each one near the top of the map. Then identify the input requirements for the first chunk. (Remember: The first chunk is a customer of the value-stream supplier.) Continue determining input requirements for each of the remaining chunks.

St. Luke's—Match Output to Customer Requirements

St. Luke's determined three distinct chunks in the ED value stream—gather information, examine, and treat—and then identified input requirements necessary for each of the chunks to proceed (see page 69).

Guideline 2a: Develop continuous flow wherever possible.

Continuous flow means that work is predictably progressing without delay. Studies of process efficiency repeatedly have proven that continuous flow (i.e., complete one task, then move the work forward to the next step with no queue or delay) is more efficient than other methods for progressing work (for example, large batch processing). You should try to achieve continuous flow everywhere you can.

In healthcare, especially in patient-care processes, it's rarely possible to achieve continuous flow through an entire value stream. It is, however, possible to achieve continuous flow through some of the chunks of the value stream and to reduce or eliminate delays between and inside processes. There are several methods—countermeasures—you can use to improve flow within your value stream. (A countermeasure is a change you initiate to address a problem.) Examine the applicability of each method in the following sequence:

1. Eliminate/combine processes

Look at all the individual process boxes involved in producing each of the major deliverables (the handoffs between chunks) in your value stream, and see if some of those boxes can be combined or even eliminated. For example, nurses who are

St. Luke's—Match Output to Customer Requirements

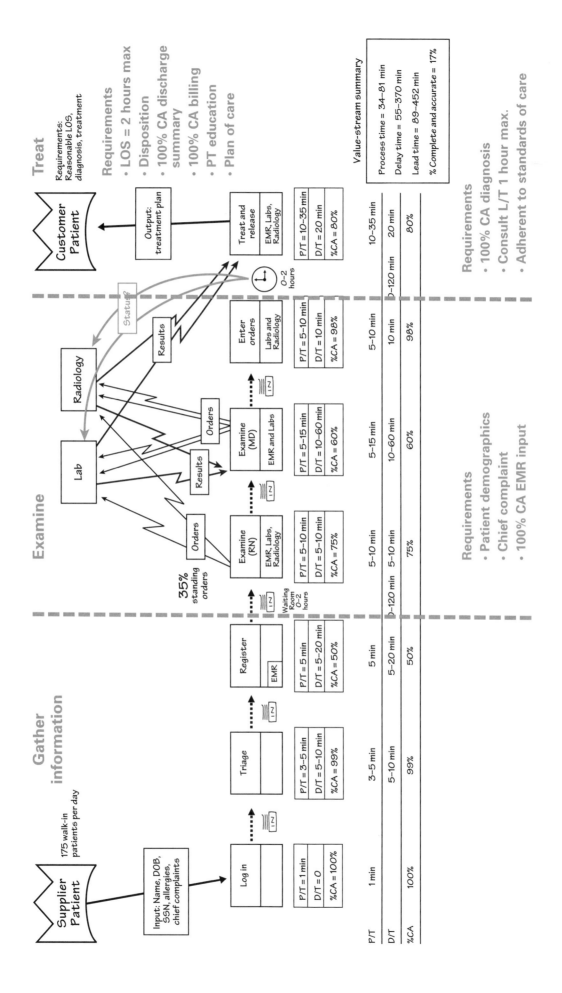

starting IVs can draw blood samples at the same time, eliminating the need for Lab personnel to come to the ED to do the draw (as well as the need for a second stick). Or staff may be authorized to follow standing orders as a way to eliminate certain approvals.

2. Make processes concurrent

Look for processes that can be performed simultaneously rather than sequentially. For example, colocating staff members with different functions who can perform their work at the same time (e.g., registration and triage) can reduce delays for your patients.

3. Flex staff to demand

Determine whether cross-training staff will free up some resources and give you greater flexibility to address major fluctuations in work volume. For example, cross-training patient registration and finance clerks to enter patient-registration information at the beginning of the process and to collect copays at the end of the process gives you more options for fluctuations in patient demand, allowing you to pull one or the other when needed.

4. Resequence

Can resequencing processes—moving them forward or backward— reduce delays? For example, involving a radiologic technologist early in the imaging process to identify special setup requirements needed by individual patients who may be immobile or require oversized equipment can prevent delays due to rework on equipment set up late in the process.

Sometimes you will want to limit the extent of continuous flow—for example, where you share resources with other processes (e.g., the same nurse treats one patient and discharges another) or with other value streams (i.e., Radiology supports both the ED and the medical floors). For shared resources, consider using *service-level agreements* (SLAs) to create predictable work progress and minimize delays. A service-level agreement is an agreement between customer and supplier processes to meet certain targets. SLAs involving targets for time most frequently address leadtime—the supplier process "agrees" to do something within a certain amount of time (see *Service-Level Agreements* on page 71).

Service-Level Agreements

A service-level agreement (SLA) governs some aspect of a handoff. A commonly used SLA governs the timing of the handoff and includes some type of time buffer. For example, an SLA with a fixed-time buffer might be, "Radiology agrees to a one-hour turnaround for all standard chest film requests." The fixed-time buffer means that some orders might be completed faster than an hour but that *all* standard chest film requests would be completed within the one-hour turnaround. Alternately, a standard-pace SLA could specify the actual timing of the handoff, such as "Housekeeping agrees to submit any stockout requests by 3 p.m. each day."

A more complex type of SLA is known as "proceed until halted"—sometimes called "no news is good news." In this type of SLA, a person who would need to approve work is informed that work is proceeding through one or more processes (e.g., "We're checking the insurance coverage of patient Doe"), and the work continues to progress in parallel while waiting approval. Within a predetermined period of time (specified in the SLA), the approver can stop the work. If the set period of time has elapsed and the work has not been stopped, it indicates that the approver has given tacit approval (the approver also can directly indicate approval).

A proceed-until-halted SLA usually requires some changes in how work is done in order to ensure that quality is built in. That's because approvals abound in cultures where "authority" for decision-making is relegated to particular individuals. Approvals cause delays, as everyone waits for the "approver" to decide, and they also reflect a perception by the approver that people cannot be trusted to do the work properly (whether justified or not). To allay concerns about competency and provide the approvers with confidence the work will be correct, work changes— such as self-checking, templates, periodic inspection of work—can be incorporated. Proceed-unless-halted agreements are typically reserved for situations where an error could be dramatic (e.g., in the ED, using standard orders to initiate treatments or order meds for patients with specific conditions prior to physician contact with the patient).

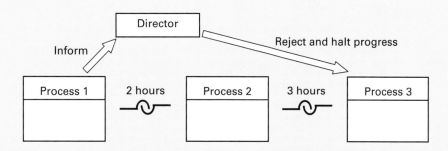

Proceed-Until-Halted SLA: Inform and continue to move the process forward.

Questions 2a: Where can you establish continuous flow? Where can you improve flow using SLAs?

Your first and simplest answer to this question is eliminating processes. If you can eliminate any processes, just put an "X" through the process box on your map. Once you have thoroughly explored opportunities to eliminate processes, consider ways to improve flow via combined or concurrent processes, cross-trained staff, and/or resequenced processes. If you can perform processes simultaneously, on your map you can "X" out the box you plan to move and draw another on top of the process with which it will be performed simultaneously. Or you can combine processes by putting an "X" over one of the processes and relabeling the remaining process, showing both in the same process box.

The mapping icon to indicate continuous flow is simply one process box next to another process box with no inbox or other icon representing a buildup of work in between the two processes. If you cannot establish continuous flow or if it is not desirable, look for places you can establish SLAs (e.g., to improve turnaround time or delivery time). Indicate the location of the SLAs on your map and add a kaizen burst symbol with an explanation for each change you plan to make.

St. Luke's Moves to Establish Flow

Although eliminating processes is not possible for St. Luke's, the team can combine and colocate processes. St. Luke's will combine triage and mini-registration, and place a full registration process together with the examination. On St. Luke's map on page 73, the ⊘ symbol indicates that there will be no inbox delay in the future state.

The team at St. Luke's has also decided to develop an SLA with the Lab and Radiology. The SLA will make clear the responsibilities for who does what. It will indicate when and how the handoffs will take place. The SLA symbol is normally used to show SLAs between different processes. However, the symbol is not used in this instance because the Lab and Radiology are not part of the ED treat-and-release value stream and the change extends beyond the scope of this project. Instead the kaizen burst has been marked to indicate that SLAs will be developed over time with Lab and Radiology.

St. Luke's Moves to Establish Flow

Guideline 2b: Define how the progression of work will be signaled where continuous flow is not possible.

There are many circumstances where continuous flow is not possible and, as noted before, some places where it may not be desirable. It's especially difficult to create continuous flow when there is a lot of variation in the way the work arrives. If new work arrives and the people doing the work act immediately—before completing the work already on hand—those workers will be overburdened *and* all the downstream processes will be delayed (think "bottleneck"). Picture one person rushing up to another and saying, "Can you squeeze this in right now," and the ramifications on all the other work.

In lean systems, the ideal is to insulate processes from the unevenness in workflow that is caused by variation in the arrival of work. To do this, it is necessary to define the:

• Specific point where the work is released to the next process, and

• Specific signal the next process will use when it is ready to receive work from the previous process. (The lean term for this arrangement is a "pull system," in which the downstream process controls when work is released to it from the upstream process.)

In doing this, the underlying assumption is that *no work progresses to the next process until the next process is ready to receive it* and has signaled that it is ready to receive it. In the ED, the boundary between triage and treatment provides a perfect example. If the triage nurse sends a patient back to a room where there's still another patient there waiting to be discharged, there's obviously no place for the new patient and no one available to begin the patient's assessment. To avoid that kind of overlap, the treatment area needs a clear, simple, and consistent method to signal triage that a room has been cleared, staff is available to transport the patient, and a member of staff is ready to receive another patient.

There also are situations where parallel independent processes are producing outputs that are required for a downstream process to perform its work (e.g., both Radiology and Lab are generating diagnostic test results for the physician who ordered them). At the very least you need to establish a mechanism for ensuring that the customer process knows that *all* of the input processes have been completed and that it is OK to proceed. If a physician orders imaging studies and lab tests, there should be a clear signal to the physician that *all* tests have been completed and *all* the results are now available in the ED so that the rest of the patient assessment can proceed.

Question 2b: How will you signal work to progress to the next process where continuous flow is not possible?

Look at your map and determine where continuous flow is not possible. Then determine where upstream processes need to be alerted so they can release work to the next process when the next process is ready. Once you have determined where you need work-progress signals, you need to decide how you will provide the signal.

Sometimes this question can be answered through your IT system (e.g., an on-screen display that indicates a patient room is empty, ready for the next patient, and a staff member is available to see the patient). In other cases, you can resort to lower-tech alternative (e.g., using a phone or two-way radio to signal that the next process is ready when staff working in two areas are unable to see each other). Or simple color-coding of information on clipboards can be used to signal that all test results are complete and available for review.

On your map, determine where the signaling needs to take place, insert a signal symbol, and add a kaizen burst indicating the need to develop an appropriate signaling system.

signal

St. Luke's Signal Work

St. Luke's did not address this issue on the map. If the team had, their map would show a signal icon between the new quick triage/miniregistration process and the combined registration/examination process so that the triage nurse would know when to send people back. In addition, the team would add a traffic light signal for results coming back from Lab, Radiology, or other places where there is no continuous flow.

Guideline 2c: Level resource capacity to address changes in the type or volume of work.

Leveling resource capacity (for example, number of staff) is a way to reduce both over-burden and unevenness in the system. Whenever you experience changes in the type or volume of work that needs to be performed in a process, consider whether that means that some resources need to be reallocated to keep the work flowing. One example, previously cited, is that of cross-training Patient Registration and Finance clerks so that personnel could be reallocated to meet an influx of new patients or a surge of patients to be discharged.

Similarly, using both registration personnel (after cross-training) and phlebotomists to do order-entry for blood draws can free up the phlebotomists to focus on the actual blood draws when multiple patients simultaneously need blood drawn.

Another kind of leveling capacity would be assessing the number of level 1, 2, and/or 3 patients and the number of level 4 and/or 5 patients that nurses (or physicians) can safely care for at the same time, and then using that information to determine to whom an additional patient gets assigned. To make these kinds of adjustments to capacity, there needs to be a signal that alerts someone when an adjustment is needed. For example, the typical ED whiteboard could be adjusted to include patient severity levels as well as room and staff assignments. This new visual would enable the triage nurse to quickly tell when adjustments are required as new patients are admitted, especially if you include a signal for "surge." Just remember that if you are using a signaling system to alert staff to a surge in patients, there also needs to be a standardized way to signal when the surge is over.

Question 2c. How will you level resource capacity?

Look at your map and determine where you will need to make changes to the usual process as variation occurs in the work. For example, where will you need to reallocate personnel, space, or equipment to adapt to changes in patient volume or acuity, and how you will know that a change in the normal condition has taken place? Consider also where you can reallocate staff when the patient volume increases or decreases—for example, moving other staff from a high-acuity stream to a lower-acuity stream when the patient volume in the two areas changes. You also should determine where you can reallocate patients to other units while assuring the unit has the necessary equipment and trained personnel (e.g., moving patients from the cardiac unit to telemetry).

Where you have made the decision to reallocate resources to level the load, indicate the future change with a leveling symbol.

load leveling

St. Luke's Leveling Work

St. Luke's has laid the groundwork for leveling by creating a separate team for treat and release. The team built in flexibility by adjusting the patient volumes that specific team members treat according to patient volume by acuity during the course of a shift.

Guideline 3: Establish stability and built-in quality with work standards and standardized work.

When processes are unstable (e.g., when patient volume increases and/or staff availability decreases) continuous flow is interrupted due to bottlenecks. If you cannot depend on a process to deliver service reliably at a certain rate, you will have delays that cause some people to be starved of work while others scramble to get back on track. It also will be difficult to determine if you have a problem and from where in the value stream it might be originating. Stable processes mean predictability.

One of the typical sources of instability relates to quality standards for work—either they don't exist or they are not consistently enforced. *Work standards* refer to the quality of the results of a process but not how the work is performed. For example, many doctors have a preference for how they take a patient history. Some prefer a conversational format, one that allows them to adjust how they take the history from each patient. Others prefer to work from a preset series of questions. The history is not judged by which method the doctor uses, but rather by the comprehensiveness of the history. Does it include all the key elements that are needed to help decide what tests might be needed and how to tailor a plan of care to the individual patient? When quality standards have not been defined and assured, rework and workarounds become part of the usual way of operating as staff members have to deal with missing or incorrect information.

In addition to ensuring work standards are met, it's important to address what goes on inside the process in order to avoid or minimize variations in work quality and reliability to get as close to 100% completeness and accuracy every time. You can achieve this condition through implementing *standardized work* and *quality at the source*.

Standardized (or standard) work incorporates specifications for how work is to be performed in order to ensure work is done according to the established current best method, regardless of who is doing the work. The current best method means that it is the best way to ensure an error-free output with the least amount of waste. The American Red Cross and American Heart Association guidelines for performing CPR are examples of standardized work familiar to healthcare providers and staff.

Poor quality of the entire value stream is generally hard to miss as it results in a bad output and lost or irate customers (and, in healthcare, unsafe conditions for patients and staff, increased rates of infection, unplanned readmissions, patient deaths, and potential litigation). However, quality problems inside the value stream are often hidden or offset by rework and firefighting. Where heroics are frequent, correcting poor quality has either become part of the process or is assured through duplication of effort at greater cost.

It is important to be able to identify a quality problem soon after it originates. The longer the delay between the source of a quality problem and its detection, the more costly it is to fix because more of people's time has been consumed and the ramifications for the patients and/or other people working in the value stream are more severe.

Quality is built into a lean value stream by first establishing clear standards that define quality for the value stream and each of its component processes and incorporating *quality at the source*—ensuring that errors are not allowed to be passed downstream. The best way to build in quality is to ensure completeness and accuracy of inputs and implement mistake-proofing countermeasures in your processes. Mistake-proofing refers to the practice of using specific techniques to make it impossible to make a mistake or to catch mistakes before they become errors.

A common example of mistake-proofing is the use of electronic computer forms that check for completeness of entry before data is submitted and passed to the next process. An incorrect data entry (mistake or missing data) is detected before the wrong (or missing) information is passed forward and incorporated into an analysis that results in an incorrect conclusion (error). Simple forms, templates, and checklists (for example, in Surgical Supply and the OR) are often used in addition to mistake-proofing to improve quality within the value stream. These are all examples of standards. Standards allow you to measure quality, easily determine abnormal from normal conditions, and ensure that the output you are passing to the next work process is truly complete and accurate.

Techniques for Quality at the Source

- Posted procedures and checklists (for both work steps and quality requirements)
- Self checking (visual confirmations built into work sequence)
- Successive checking (following process checks)
- Mistake proofing (automatic error detection)
- Zone control (checks before leaving the group or area)
- Product checks (final or functional inspection)
- Systems for immediately giving feedback about abnormalities to the processes where they originated

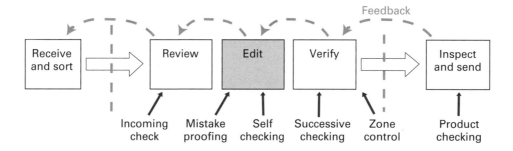

Standardized Work Is Not Built-in Monotony

Many people view standardized work as "great for others, but not really appropriate for what I do." They will resist application of standardized work to their activities even while recognizing that it provides the following benefits:

- Applies a consistency of approach for all people who do the work, which enables job rotation and ability to balance workloads;

- Reduces or eliminates the need for job descriptions;

- Enables the use of visual management to surface problems that everyone can see;

- Offers a baseline for continuous improvement;

- Ensures stability by enabling quality in the process and predictability of timing.

But why the resistance? Many people, including professionals working in health-care settings, view their jobs as requiring creativity because every time they work the conditions are different. "We can't have standards here, no two patients are alike!" The standardized work skeptics also form a mental image of workers in a factory being told what to do ("behaving like robots"), performing the same repetitive motions over and over again.

This misperception runs counter to lean principles in two ways. First, a core lean principle is that it is just as important to improve work as it is to do the work. Second, the people who do the work are the only ones who can own the improve-ments for their work. Standardized work locks in the current best-known methods while all the people who do the work strive to think of new and better ways that they might try (as controlled experiments) in the future. If these new ways are determined to be better through careful observation and measurement, then the standards are updated. Standardized work is just a baseline (the control group) in an experiment that allows people to make things better and share their learning across the organization.

Rather than resisting standardized work, ask yourself, "Where can we standardize? What is appropriate to standardize? Where will a standard provide benefit to the value stream and ultimately the customer?"

At each process or chunk you must have the means to ensure quality and:

• Prevent incomplete/inaccurate input,

• Prevent mistakes,

• Recognize problems in output easily before you pass them along.

Question 3: Where will you use standardized work to establish stability and built-in quality?

To answer this question, you must dive into the details of each process. Consider the changes you want to make to improve the first-time quality or the completeness and accuracy of the input to each process. Look for places where staff have their own ways of performing processes (e.g., room cleanup, supply restocking, patient transfer, patient orders, documentation of findings), and determine which of those would benefit from standardized work. If standardized work is not appropriate, look for places where quality could be improved by developing work standards and ways to see that standards have been met. Indicate those changes on your map in kaizen bursts.

St. Luke's Standardized Work

St. Luke's map on page 81 shows how the team plans to institute new protocols in triage, and apply standardized work to the registration and discharge process.

Summary of Expected Results

When you have completed the markup of your current-state map—with all the changes to improve value, flow, and work—draw a "clean" version and complete the map with a summary of the expected metrics. This is now your future-state map. But it is still a draft susceptible to change based on the feedback you receive when you will socialize it.

St. Luke's ED Treat and Release—Future-State Map

St. Luke's future-state map illustrates the proposed changes without the clutter of the current-state map (see pages 82–83). Notice the timeline has been added as well as the box of summary measures. Adding metrics will be discussed in Chapter 5.

St. Luke's Standardized Work

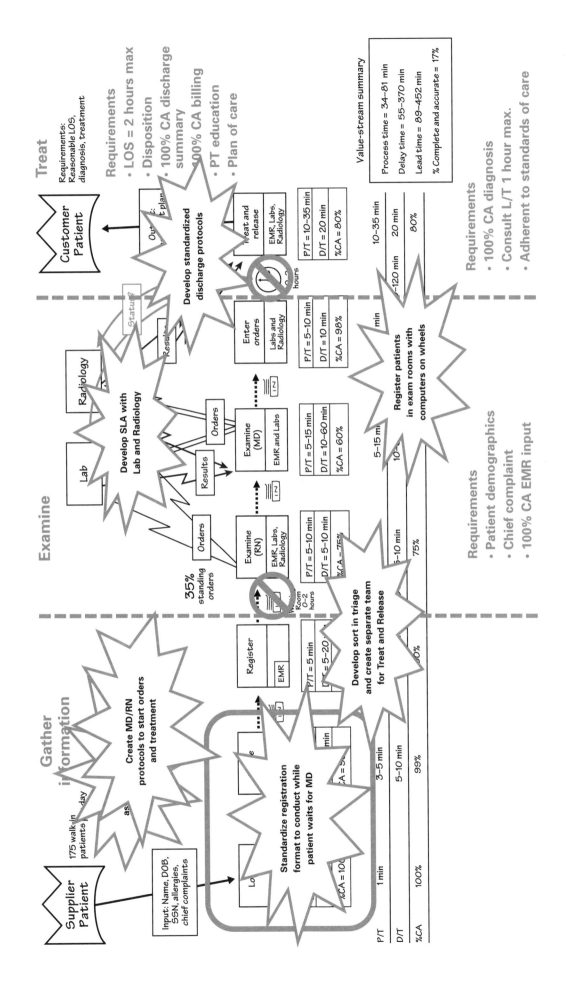

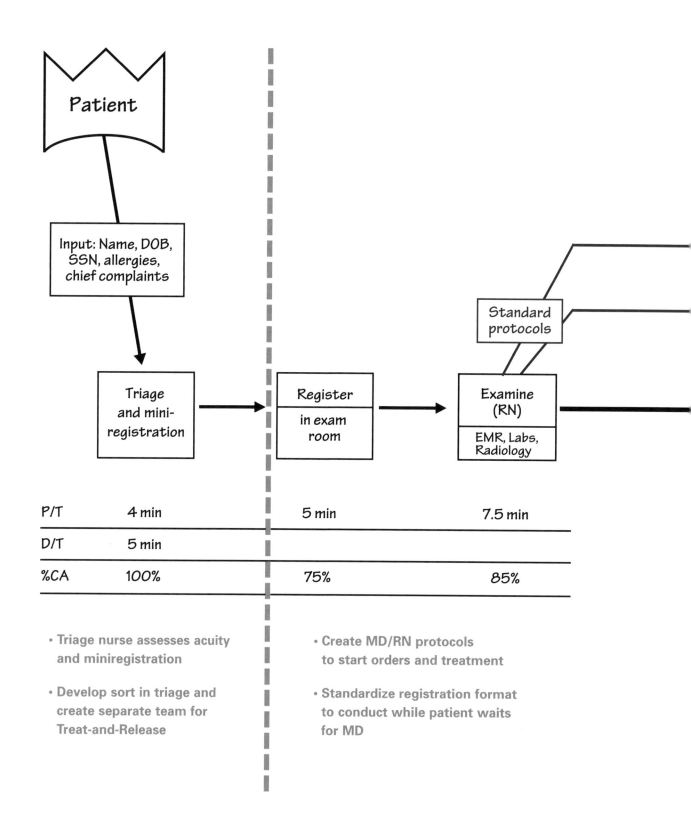

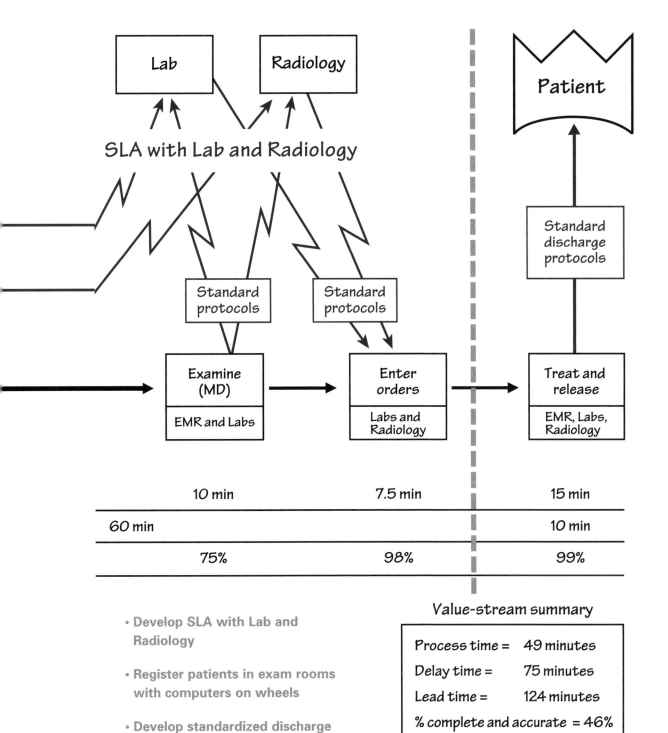

Lab	Radiology			Patient

SLA with Lab and Radiology

Standard protocols

Standard protocols

Standard discharge protocols

Examine (MD)	Enter orders	Treat and release
EMR and Labs	Labs and Radiology	EMR, Labs, Radiology

10 min	7.5 min	15 min
60 min		10 min
75%	98%	99%

- Develop SLA with Lab and Radiology

- Register patients in exam rooms with computers on wheels

- Develop standardized discharge protocols

Value-stream summary

Process time =	49 minutes
Delay time =	75 minutes
Lead time =	124 minutes
% complete and accurate = 46%	

Socializing the Future State

Now that you have a future-state map, it's time to socialize it. The word "map" in this case is a good but incomplete metaphor. Your future state is the destination you hope to achieve, but it does not tell you how you are going to get there. You'll need a plan for that, and that's the topic of the next chapter. However, before you can have a plan for how to get somewhere, everyone involved must understand what may occur, be given an opportunity to comment on the plan, and then agree on where to go. This agreement on the destination is what you are building toward as you socialize the map.

Socializing a future state is often more difficult than socializing the current state and problems. The difficulty sometimes occurs because anyone who was not part of the conversation in which you identified the problems that need to be addressed and/or a member of the team that created the future-state map may feel left out. Help the stakeholders understand the guidelines for a lean value stream and walk them through the future-state questions with an explanation of how you arrived at the changes. If possible, reference back to observations that they had made when you shared the current state, reminding them of what existed and why it needs to change.

It can also be helpful to bring and review the marked up current-state map, lean value proposition, and problem list before sharing the future-state map. This action provides context for the changes you're proposing. Remind colleagues that the future-state map is not about developing new processes or procedures (yet). Rather, it is a way to define and execute some simple experiments, in which they may be involved, to see how the value stream can be improved. This will set the expectation that some experiments will inevitably fail (and in lean that is not a bad thing when it promotes learning) and that each experiment will be communicated during the next phase of the project.

Finally, perform PDCA on your socialization methods. What have you learned about socialization from your previous attempts? What changes do you want to make for this phase that incorporate those lessons learned?

Presentation to Senior Leadership

Once you've fully socialized your future-state map (including input from your leadership team) and made revisions, if necessary, you will formally present your future-state vision to senior leadership to get an "agree to proceed" response. Give yourself about an hour to briefly review your problem statement, value proposition, current-state map and metrics, your problem list, and your future-state map. Allow time for leadership to ask questions about your proposed future state.

Who makes the presentation will depend on your staff availability. The greatest learning results when all members of the improvement team attend the meeting and participate in making the presentation and responding to questions. It's also helpful if someone (typically, the lean champion) meets briefly with senior leadership just prior to the presentation. He or she should explain the purpose of the presentation and reinforce that one of the two main goals is to help your staff learn the lean methodology for problem solving. That means that it's important for senior leadership to be supportive of the team as they attempt for the first time to tackle a value-stream improvement project.

Senior leaders are encouraged to ask questions about the process the team followed to arrive at their recommendations and to clarify the recommendations themselves. However, as a general guideline, senior leaders should be asked not to offer different solutions. Senior leadership's focus should be how the group thought about the solution to problems, whether the group appears to have a grasp on solving the identified current-state problems, and whether the proposed solution is a reasonable start. In this way, they are beginning to nurture and develop a problem-solving culture. Unless senior leadership truly cannot support the recommendations made by the team, the expectation is that they will give the team the go ahead and support their efforts to work together to improve the value stream and to learn by careful experimentation.

Storytelling Power of a Map

It is often surprising how easy it is to articulate improvement visions to senior leadership and gain support based on presentation of current- and future-state maps. Many times these visions include ideas that have been suggested in the past but have fallen on deaf ears. This time, however, the ideas are quickly grasped with just a high-level glance and embraced and supported. What is different?

The answer is certainly dependent on the unique cultures of each organization, but the use of value-stream mapping sets the team up for success by first involving the leadership in the problem definition (selection and scoping). The team has the current-state map, which provides a medium for telling the story of the current situation with pictures, data, and facts. The future-state vision generates less resistance than typical proposals because the leadership has already agreed that there are problems worth addressing, and the team has done a rigorous investigation and analysis that is clearly evident in the maps.

Chapter 5
Measuring the Future State and Planning for Change

This chapter will help you and your team:

• Create a way to measure the future state.

• Develop an improvement plan that translates proposed changes into goals and actions.

• Learn how to conduct experiments.

• Communicate and delegate actions.

• Prepare to manage change.

Chapter 5
Measuring the Future State and Planning for Change

Turning Vision into Action

You now have a *shared vision* of the actual results your team expects to achieve. To achieve those results—move from the current state to the future state—change will be necessary. Your team has begun to identify those changes, but will now need to translate them into clearly stated goals and actions (i.e., the means) to achieve those goals. You also will socialize the actions with those who need to take action (a group much broader than the improvement team) and create a way to measure progress.

Because there is never a guarantee that your proposed actions will produce the results you want, in this chapter you also will learn how to trial actions in a series of experiments and to observe what happens, learn what works and what doesn't, and then adjust your approach as required. This section of the guide walks you through how to create your improvement plan, including establishing goals and action plans, and how to socialize this effort.

Measuring the Future State

You concluded your future-state mapping by summarizing your metrics and presenting your vision to senior leadership. Before you proceed any further, take a reality check. Spend a little more time checking your metrics with a comparison table.

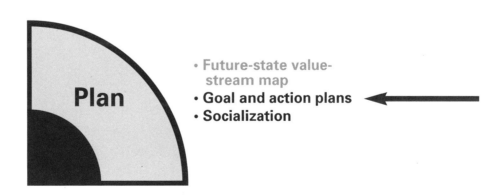

Current State vs. Future State Comparison

Metric	Current state (actual)	Future state (planned)
Total process time		
Total delay time		
Total leadtime		
Composite percent complete and accurate		
Other (e.g., FTEs)		

1. Estimate your future-state metrics using the same metric categories you used for the current-state map (e.g., process time, delay time, and percent complete and accurate) and enter the metrics in the data boxes on your future-state map (see St. Luke's future-state map on pages 82–83).

2. Total your estimates for each of these key metrics on your future-state map.

3. Compare your future-state metrics with current-state metrics.

Remember several points regarding your current- and future-state results. First, your current-state metrics may have been estimates. If you did not get feedback during socialization about the accuracy of those current-state estimates, you will need to get that feedback or validate the estimates through actual observation. Make sure that someone on the improvement team observes the process directly and takes sample measurements that are representative enough to give you a good baseline.

Second, when calculating the total process time, determine whether understanding staff capacity is important. If your problem statement involves resource utilization and staffing levels, you may need to better understand capacity. If so, document the total number of personnel involved as well as the process time.

You can capture total resources in two ways:

- Total work hours across all shifts for the particular process for all customers divided by 8 hours. The result is typically expressed in full-time equivalents (FTEs).

- Process time per customer as well as the total number of people who do the work and the percentage of time they have available for the work (e.g., 10 minutes/patient across four nurses, 10% available).

Third, make sure you are not double counting delay time inside process time and/or double counting delays. If you have delays both between and inside process boxes on your map, you want to make sure that these delays are truly separate delays and they warrant being added together. Because length of stay is such an important metric for clinical value streams, it is critical to understand the delays accurately if you are to have any chance of making improvements.

Finally, when you review percent complete and accurate (%CA), remember that this metric concerns the input to a process, not how well the process is performing. If you are interested in measuring the quality of a process' output, you can use the downstream process %CA, or you can add an additional checkpoint and metric for the quality of the output. For example, you might have a defined objective to reduce sentinel events, which are obviously a measure of output quality (or lack thereof) and which can be tracked for each process.

In addition, you may need to revisit your future-state metrics if changes were made in work, flow, processes or methods during socialization. Your current-state metrics will need updating if you altered your project scope in moving from the current state to future state (i.e., you are no longer comparing the same process across the two maps). If that is the case, to make an apples-to-apples comparison of future state to current state you'll have to recalculate the current-state summary metrics.

You always want to ask yourself at every stage of this project if there's something you have learned along the way that needs to be communicated quickly to avoid confusion and delays in gaining agreement among all stakeholders. And if your answer is "yes," you want to provide the appropriate updates in the maps and in socializing.

Planning for Improvement

You need to be strategic and systematic about how you initiate change. Be prepared that, even with a carefully developed plan, your actions and methods may not work as you intended or produce the results you hoped to achieve. For that reason, lean approaches change as a series of experiments designed to produce learning about what works best to achieve the outcomes you desire.

As you learned in Chapter 1, the fundamental tool for producing learning is the scientific method—specifically the PDCA cycle. To practice the scientific method, you need a hypothesis to test. The changes you want to make and the expected outcomes due to those changes form your hypotheses. The steps you are going to follow to implement the changes and test the outcomes are your experiments—the *plan* of PDCA. Experimentation occurs as you try to implement the changes and see what happens, assess what you've learned, and apply the learning to get closer to your future state.

As with all good experiments, careful planning prior to action is key to producing results that are valid and reliable. In this case the planning involves identifying the results you hope to achieve, the changes you are going to initiate to try to get those results, and the actions you will take to make and validate the changes:

- *Results* are the improvements in the performance of your value stream. Results are captured in your project objective and your future-state metrics.

- *Changes* are the process or procedure improvements you will initiate to close gaps between your current and future states. Changes are primarily represented by the kaizen bursts on your future-state map and indicate that *something* must be done. Changes must be translated to goals with targets, which enables your team to plan actions and track progress.

- *Actions* are the specific activities (the yet-to-be determined *something)* that the team and other stakeholders will perform to initiate the changes. Experiments are used to validate proposed actions and your progress toward goals and targets.

How do you plan experiments? First, understand the changes required of the end-to-end value stream in order to get the desired results. What would such a change mean at the value-stream chunk and process level? Go back to the business, clinical, or customer-service objectives for the project, and examine your original problem statement and project objective(s) on the lean value proposition.

Now compare your two maps: the problems identified on the current-state map and the changes implied and/or described by the future-state map (the kaizen bursts). Make a list of the changes, and check them against your original purpose: "Will these changes address the original problems?" or "If we make these changes, will we meet the objectives on the value proposition?" If the answer is "no," you will need to revise your scope and objective (and justify that change to your stakeholders) or modify the changes you have selected to fit your original scope and objective. Where the answer is "yes," you've identified your targets for kaizen and where experiments will take place.

Scientific Method and Value-Stream Improvement

Scientific Method	Value-Stream Improvement
Define the question Gather information (observe)	Grasp the situation/problem, investigate cause, select countermeasure
Form hypothesis	Plan for implementing and testing
Perform experiment and collect results	Do
Analyze results	Check
Interpret results and draw conclusions that serve as a basis for new hypotheses	Act/Adjust

 repeat

You'll probably find that you've identified many changes that you will need to make to address your problems. Since the first round of improvements should take 60 to 120 days, making all the changes may not be possible. If you identified more than five changes to get you to your future state, prioritize your improvements and select the five to address in your first round (see *Tips for Prioritizing Changes to Your Future State* on page 92).

St. Luke's High-Level Changes

St. Luke's case is illustrative of the types of changes that are typical in a value-stream improvement project (lasting approximately 90 days). The proposed changes to create St. Luke's future state are described on *St. Luke's High-Level Changes* map on page 93.

Tips for Prioritizing Changes to Your Future State

If your team selected a problem and scope that may take more than a year to achieve, you probably have a long list of changes to consider. Before you go further, figure out which ones to tackle first. Here are some suggestions to help you do that:

1) Limit your first round to three to five changes, which is the maximum amount of change work most teams can achieve in 60–120 days.

2) Combine, if possible, changes that can be addressed as a single project.

3) As a team, create an agreed-to list of criteria to use in prioritizing the changes. The following questions will help set your criteria:

   • Where are you likely to have a good chance of success? A quick success will increase future cooperation and commitment inside and outside your improvement team.

   • How evenly are the changes you want to make distributed across the value stream? Make sure you don't overburden some parts of your team and leave others waiting for months to get involved. Consider that multiple changes simultaneously in the same part of the value stream will make it difficult to determine which of the changes is producing the impact you observe.

   • Is there a logical order (e.g., a critical pathway) for tackling the changes? Do some changes need to take place first to enable you to enact other changes?

   • Can you make the changes with the resources available to you?

   • How can you incorporate changes that make the work less burdensome to staff and changes that directly address your problem statement and objective? (Remember, staff members are more likely to stay committed and enthusiastic if they also see some direct benefit from the first round of improvements.)

4) Once you've generated your criteria, apply them to your list of changes and see if your team can reach consensus. Then socialize your list of criteria and your proposed list of changes to come up with your final list of changes you want to address in the next 60–120 days.

St. Luke's High-Level Changes

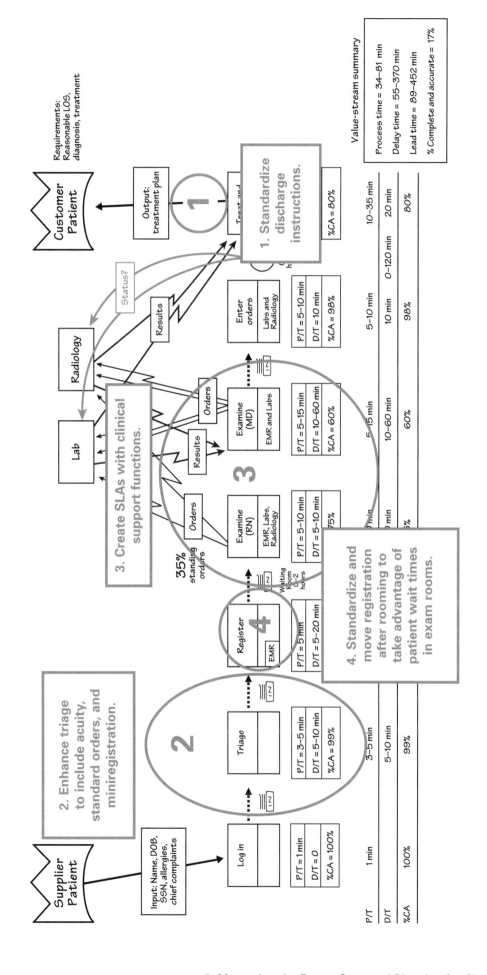

Developing Improvement Goals

Now that your team has prioritized their proposed changes and selected the ones they want to address first, the next task is to turn these proposed changes into formal *improvement goals*. Keep in mind that goals are not actions. Goals are the outcomes or results you want when you complete your implementation of the future state (i.e., your hypothesis for what's needed). Actions are the steps you take to try to achieve the outcome or result (i.e., the experiments to see if the hypothesis is working).

You and your team will need to commit to the outcomes you want to achieve—your goals—not just the actions you plan to take. To stay focused on outcomes and to ensure that each outcome relates to your overall objectives, link the change you plan to make with the specific purpose for making the change (i.e., a specific impact you want to achieve on the performance of your value stream).

Improvement goals = change in value stream + purpose

When creating goal statements, pay careful attention to the wording. Remember that these goals need to be socialized, and they also must stand on their own. Each goal statement should be clearly understood by someone who is not part of the core team that created the future state. During the socialization process, encourage stakeholders to ask questions when the wording or reason for change is unclear.

St. Luke's Goals

In practice, adding the phrase "in order to" helps convert a change into a goal statement. Here is how St. Luke's proposed changes convert to inprovement goals.

Change in value stream	Purpose
1. Standardize D/C instruction	+ *in order to* decrease the % of readmissions
2. Enhance triage role to include acuity, standard orders and miniregistration	+ *in order to* start treatment sooner for certain protocols
3. Develop SLAs with clinical support functions	+ *in order to* eliminate rework, reduce D/T, and start treatment more quickly
4. Standardize and move registration after rooming to take advantage of waiting time in exam rooms	+ *in order to* reduce overall length of stay

---

Improvements can stall or fail because the change and/or intent is misunderstood by those stakeholders who must buy into the change. For that reason, the facilitator and process owner should each take a lead role to ensure the goal statements are effective and not misunderstood. The facilitator can provide an outside perspective to ensure clarity, and the process owner can provide direction to ensure that the goal statements support the high-level problem being addressed by the project scope. Jointly they can help coach the goal owners to write statements that are clear, specific, and unambiguous.

Identify Goal Owners

To complete the goal statements, the team should identify owners and targets for each goal. Every goal needs an owner who was involved in creating the future-state vision. The goal owner is responsible for ensuring that the goal is achieved at the target levels to be agreed upon by the team. Of course, a goal cannot be accomplished by any one individual. Goal ownership means getting the necessary support, either from key stakeholders or those directly affected. The goal owner also is responsible for reporting on progress toward the targets. If progress is below target, goal ownership means leading problem solving around the situation to develop countermeasures to get it on track.

If some of the changes your team identified involve systems or processes outside your value stream, you may need to select a goal owner from outside the value stream or familiar with the external system or process. For example, if you want to shift responsibilities for some blood draws in the ED from phlebotomy to nursing, you may need a goal owner from Laboratory Services. If changes involving the Lab were part of your original project scope, you ideally will have included representation from the Lab on your improvement team. If not, you will need to choose someone on the team who can work effectively with the Lab to get the desired changes made.

Define Goal Targets

Once your improvement team has goals and goal owners for their prioritized value-stream improvements, they will need to state clear and specific targets for each. Targets include the measurable or observable impacts of the changes along with the timing necessary for achieving the impacts. Targets answer the questions, "How do you know you have achieved the goal?" and "When do you expect to see results?"

To set your goal targets, ask:

- What you are going to measure?

- How much change you expect to see?

- When do you expect the change(s) to occur?

Each goal owner is responsible for setting the targets, but nothing is done in isolation. The goal owner must get agreement from the other stakeholders on the targets and then measure and communicate progress relative to the targets to the rest of the team and to those working in the value stream.

If you are working with goals that involve developing policies, procedures, and/or protocols, the target also should describe the level of performance you expect to achieve by your target date. For example, if you want to implement a new procedure, you need to decide whether you plan to:

- Draft and trial the procedure in a series of small, reversible experiments (number of trials by target date),

- Train personnel on the revised procedure (number of persons trained by target date),

- Ensure personnel can perform the procedure at an acceptable level of proficiency (number of employees proficient by target date),

- Ensure that personnel are routinely following the new procedure (X% of compliance by target date).

St. Luke's Goals and Targets
Some of the targets identified by St. Luke's are quantitative: they contain a metric as well as a threshold of performance and a due date. Some of the targets are qualitative: they are simply the establishment of something such as a protocol or a particular deliverable with a due date. In such cases the target is assumed to be 100%.

Goals	Targets
1. Standardize D/C instructions in order to decrease the % of readmissions	• Reduce readmissions by 50% • Trial complete by Aug. 15
2. Enhance triage role to include acuity, standard orders, and miniregistration in order to start treatment sooner for certain protocols	• MD/RN protocols established by June 1 • Triage staff fully trained by June 30 • Evidence of protocols in use on all shifts by Aug. 15
3. Create SLAs with clinical support functions to eliminate rework, reduce D/T, and start treatment more quickly	• Reports for x-rays in less than 30 minutes • SLAs in use by Aug. 30
4. Standardize and move registration after rooming to take advantage of waiting time in exam rooms in order to reduce overall LOS	• Reduce door-to-doc time by 10 minutes by Aug. 15 • Increase patient satisfaction by 2% by Aug. 15

Learning for Improvement through 'Small, Reversible Experiments'

When teams try to make improvements, they usually encounter or surface obstacles. Actions and methods likely will need correction along the way to achieving your goals (many experiments fail to prove the hypothesis). However, when goals have clearly defined targets, you have a guide to gauge the effectiveness of the actions. You can modify methods or take additional action as needed to remain on course to achieve the goals.

It is through this discovery process of what works, what doesn't work, and the development of new countermeasures that teams truly begin to develop the capability for continuous improvement. So many times in healthcare, improvement efforts fail because changes are forced from the outside or treated as solutions ("If we do _____ there will be no problems."). When changes are forced from the outside and they do not produce the anticipated results, the changes are easily dismissed by those doing the work because they did not originate the ideas ("I knew that wouldn't work."). In addition, when changes are treated as "solutions" and they don't work, teams are easily discouraged because of the physical and emotional investments in trying to make the solution work. The solutions have been promoted as all that is needed.

Because improvement has not been viewed as a continuous journey, people are upset when they haven't reached their target destination. However, when changes are viewed as just "small, reversible experiments" along the improvement journey, teams are freer to try new things and more willing to accept that they must try something different when the results are not what they should be. Over time the scientific method becomes ingrained into the normal routine for making improvements, and, therefore, continuous learning is taking place around the way work is done, not just the work itself.

Developing Action Plans for Each Goal

Goals and targets of your project represent agreement about what is to change. With such an agreement, it will be much easier to identify the specific methods and action steps you think will help you achieve the goals along with the corresponding action-step owners, targets, and support/resources. Targets for action steps—like targets for goals—may include both timing and quality. Action steps and action targets constitute the action plan to achieve a specific goal.

You've probably recognized by now that the value-stream improvement method, with rapid experimentation, differs significantly from traditional committee approaches to making organizational change. Both methods involve discussion and action, but the focus and timelines usually differ. *Committee work* often focuses on gaining acceptance of change by bringing all the stakeholders to the table and hashing things out, a drawn-out process that requires a great deal of politics, negotiation, and compromise to get a result that everyone can accept. *VSI work* focuses on implementing change by trying quick experiments to see what works—and what doesn't work (see *A Quick Guide to Running Experiments* on page 101).

Once a team (including the critical stakeholders) has agreed on a goal and targets, the focus turns to selecting a method to achieve the target(s), developing the action steps necessary to try out the method, checking if it produces the desired results, and then deciding what happens next. Because lean focuses on producing verifiable results before implementing change in standard work, much of the conflict over political sensitivities gets reduced. If this type of planning is new to your team, the following suggestions and steps for action planning can be helpful.

Planning suggestions

- Brainstorm the steps needed to implement the change you try. Write the steps on sticky notes and move them around until you get a complete set in a logical sequence.

- Determine who will be responsible for ensuring each action step occurs. It does not have to be a member of the improvement team. However, it should be someone who is familiar with the work to be performed, who can lead the effort, and who was involved in developing and committed to the future-state vision.

- Assign timing targets to each step. (Start from the end and work your way back to the beginning. That will ensure that you incorporate the steps into the time you have available to complete the goal.)

- Assign quality targets to steps as appropriate.

- Identify any resources/support personnel required to complete the action. Remember, you must keep your resources within your original problem scope. However, you will need to expand beyond your improvement team to include people who are doing the work involved in the action steps and, in some cases, people/groups who supply or are customers of this work. In effect, you will be creating an "action team" for each goal, such as the Discharge Group (*D/C group*) shown in the table on page 100 and other individuals or groups (*IT support, Admissions support*) as needed.

- Socialize your plan with the key stakeholders.

Steps for lean action plans

1. Define the change you want to make. Although it appears in your goal, you may need to refine it a little before you begin.

2. Identify key metrics (or data points) and begin to gather baseline data (numbers or observations) to determine how things are working now and how you will know if they improve.

3. Determine who needs to provide input into designing the change and how that information will be used.

4. Gather the necessary information.

5. Design the change.

6. Circulate the draft plan for change for review/approval and run an experiment to validate it.

7. Modify the change, if necessary.

8. Communicate the change to those who will be using it and/or provide training and evaluate competency.

9. Implement the change.

10. Monitor progress/performance.

11. Evaluate and determine next steps.

St. Luke's—Goal, Target, and Action Steps

Here is the action plan for the discharge-instructions goal for St. Luke's.

Goal, Target, and Action Steps

Goal: Develop standardized discharge instructions in order to reduce readmissions by 50%. Trial complete by August 15.

Action step/method	Responsible	Target	Support resources
1. Select group from ED that will be involved in developing new discharge Instructions	Allen	June 8	−Improvement team
2. Establish %CA baseline for discharge instructions	Allen	June 15	−D/C group
3. Group reviews existing documents and procedures for discharge	Mary	June 15	−D/C group −IT support −Admission support −D/C documents
4. Group identifies problems in existing discharge procedures	Jennifer	June 20	−D/C group −ED MDs −Admissions support
5. Develop standardized discharge documents for a trial	Allen	July 1	−D/C group −Admissions support −ED MDs −IT support
6. Develop a measuring system to evaluate the trial	Mary	July 15	−D/C group −IT support
7. Conduct a trial over an agreed-to timeframe	Allen	Aug. 8	−D/C team −ED staff −Admissions support −ED MDs
8. Evaluate results and implement, or do a retrial	Allen	Aug. 15	−D/C team

A blank action plan template and other resources are available at *lean.org/ppj*

A Quick Guide to Running Experiments

Many actions plans involve testing of new forms and procedures. If you've never run an experimental test, below are some tips to help you get started.

1. Determine the change (procedure, form, etc.) that you think will result in an improvement and draft a version that you want to test.
   - Circulate the draft for review, gathering input from people who are most likely to recognize potential problems with the change.
   - Make any needed changes.

2. Determine how you will know that the change has had the impact (result) you want (i.e., decide what you want to observe/measure).

3. Develop a step-by-step procedure (Who? What? When? Where? How?) for trialing the change.
   - Identify observers for the trial. Provide them with instructions on what to observe and how to document their observations.
   - Do a virtual run through of the pilot procedure with the people who will participate in the trial.
   - Make additional changes as needed.

4. Secure any necessary permissions to run the trial.

5. Develop an elevator speech for the experiment and inform other people who need to know. (Make sure to communicate in a way that ensures that the critical stakeholders get the information in a clear, concise, and timely way.)

6. Run the experiment.

7. Interview participants and get their feedback on what worked/what needs to change.

8. Review participant feedback and observer data and decide what happens next. Options include:
   - Repeat the experiment as designed but implement the next round during different circumstances (e.g., on night shift, during peak hours, etc.). Assess the results.
   - Revise the change and/or the procedure, repeat the experiment, and assess the results.
   - Scrap the change and try a different approach to the problem you're trying to address.
   - Implement the change as standard work, train staff to use it, and monitor results (for consistency of implementation and impact).

9. Write a summary of your results and circulate to pilot participants and key stakeholders.

Consensus and Alignment on the Improvement Plan

The truth about changing things in organizations is that none of us can do it alone, not even the CEO. Change involves interdependent and interlocking relationships. For that reason, lean practitioners define plans as sets of agreements for making change or a series of changes. And, as plans evolve, it is critical to make sure that the stakeholders remain in agreement about the desired results, the changes to be attempted, and the actions required to implement the changes.

Because socialization and communication of the plan and progress in implementing it is so critical, most teams find it helps to include the communication process formally into their plan and their system for checks and reviews. There are two primary methods to incorporate them in a plan: 1) You can include communication as an essential part of each goal, or 2) you can establish a separate goal for communication. If you decide to have a separate goal for communication, remember to use the same goal statement format (*change* + *purpose*). Whichever method you use, don't forget to include targets for the element of communication. And depending on what kind of targets you set, you may need to determine a method(s) for measuring how you will know whether you have effectively communicated and socialized your goals and actions.

Once you have drafted your initial plan you will need to determine what each stakeholder group needs to see as well as the most effective forum in which to see it and reach agreement. You then conduct socialization sessions, gathering feedback on the plan as well as how you intend to manage its implementation. Even if your work has been positively received up until now, it's not uncommon for teams to encounter resistance as they get specific about what they plan to change and how they plan to do it. For that reason, it's important to be diligent about how you socialize and communicate your plan.

When you have finished socializing the plan, set up a leadership team review. This will give the your team an opportunity to present the details of the final plan for change, how the improvement team will communicate the plan and its status, and how the project will be managed with reviews and checks.

Chapter 6
Establishing Project Management

This chapter will help you and your team:

• Ensure execution of the improvement plan (the "do" of PDCA).

• Develop a process to monitor progress.

• Focus your progress checks and reviews.

• Communicate and display progress.

• Manage, problem solve, and learn as you reinforce PDCA.

Chapter 6
Establishing Project Management

Planning to Manage Execution of the Improvement Plan

Once you and your implementation team know what you want to do (*goals*) and how you hope to do it (*actions*), you then need to develop a system to *manage* your improvement efforts. Remember, as you run experiments, you need to be able to check the results against your hypotheses. You individual experiments are part of your overall experiment—the "do" of PDCA—and you need a structure to respond to and solve problems, trial new ideas, and make changes, and learn as you make the changes.

At this *do* phase you will validate the plan by *doing* what you said you would do—or as close to that as possible—and monitoring what happens. You will check to see what you've done, reviewing and evaluating the impact. Then, based on your evaluation, decide which of the following actions you need to take next:

- Figure out how to maintain and standardize what you've achieved,
- Start over with a new plan (because the other one didn't work),
- Keep the plan but do a better job implementing it,
- Aim for more improvement by developing a new future state.

- **Measure results**
- **Visual management**
- **Problem solving**
- **Conduct reviews and checks**
- **Transition to continuous improvement**
- **Socialization**

Developing a Lean Management System

As you develop a system to manage your improvement project, think about developing measures to answer three questions:

1. Are we on schedule? (Level 1)

2. Are we doing what we said we would do the way we said we would do it? (Level 2)

3. If we are doing what we said we would do the way we said we would do it, are we having the impact we expect to achieve? (Level 3)

Developing measures of execution to plan is pretty simple. It typically involves monitoring project goals (and action plans) in a spreadsheet or Gantt chart. In contrast, developing good in-process and outcome measures may not be so easy. Your team will save time in the long run if it spends some time upfront figuring out how best to measure the results —both in-process and outcome—of the pilot tests it plans to run.

The measures you use to monitor execution must also help you solve problems. At a minimum, they need to:

• Be simple and easy to use,

• Provide direct answers (or as direct as possible) to the questions above,

• Provide answers you can trust, and

• Provide answers that are timely (available when you need them).

You will develop systems to monitor your progress in a way to answer the three key questions so you can initiate problem solving when the answer to any or all of the questions is "no." And your systems will make progress—and problems—visible.

Developing Your Measures

To help guide you in developing your measures, here are a series of questions to consider:

1. What will you measure?

Is it an output rate (e.g., number of patients discharged in two hours or less) or a quality measure (e.g., number of missing items on a form)? Think about how the measurement relates to your goal and your target. Is your proposed measure the most direct way to measure the outcome or the process efficiency?

2. How will you measure?

Is extra work required to collect the information? Is the act of measuring built into the work process? Is it easy to collect the measurements so that it will not be perceived as a burden? Are you using manual or electronic means to collect information? If electronic, will you need to work with IT to get the specific information you need? Will you have access to the results when you need them?

Measures used during experimentation can be as simple as tick marks on a single sheet of paper along with brief instructions, a date, a time, and initials or signatures. You can also simplify data collection by measuring the exceptions to your expected results. For example, rather than measuring the number of patients who are able to be roomed immediately during a particular shift, you might track only those who are not. Exception measures are particularly useful when they can be directly associated with some "correction." The number and types of corrections can be used to surface additional problems that require countermeasures in order to make progress toward your goals.

During execution, you will probably find that you need to develop most of your in-process measures and methods for collection. On the other hand, you are more likely to be able to use existing systems to obtain some of your outcome measures, especially if you have a good health information system.

3. How often will you measure and how much data is necessary to give you a (not necessarily statistically) reliable answer?

How often do you need to know the impact? Are you capturing every occurrence or a sample? What is the nature of the process? Are there natural cycles in the process or in the work that suggest particular frequency?

Again, to answer these questions, think about the type of impact you hope to have and determine how much time you can afford between surfacing problems (if the people collecting the data are problem solving) and initiating problem solving. If you need to respond quickly to problems you are surfacing, you may need to begin with a small sample size. In addition, consider how the nature of the work or work cycles impacts how long your data collection needs to continue to get the sample size you need. For example, if you are looking at improvements in patient flow, you might have several opportunities during a day or a shift to measure that flow. If, on the other hand, you are looking at improvements in restocking exam-room supplies, which are stocked only once per day, you are locked into a daily frequency for collecting data.

4. How will you measure outcomes vs. the means to achieve those outcomes?

You will need to determine how you know that the change you are proposing has been implemented effectively enough to see if it can produce the expected outcome, as well as whether the impact has occurred. You will then use the outcome measures to determine if the experiments have produced the results you expected and warrant creating new standards. Once new standards are put in place, you will then use measures of the means to ensure these new standards are being adhered to and continue to be executed as planned.

5. Who will report the data? How? How often? Where?

Just as with your goals and action plans, you need to determine who has responsibility for collecting the data and reporting it. Different types of data may require different plans. Some data should be reported to the improvement team on a weekly basis and posted on the unit where all who have participated in the collection can see the results and trends. Other data—for example, the data collected for the rapid learning experiments—should be reported immediately to the team running the experiments and then reported again to the rest of the improvement team once the experiments are concluded. Remember, sharing meaningful data frequently helps to reinforce the value of data with staff. In this setting it is often more helpful to use simple run charts to display continuous data than to report complex statistical process control (SPC) data. Finally, your data plan should identify what data needs to be reported to leadership, how often, and by what mechanism.

Who is Going to Check What, and How Often?

Hitting a target out of the gate is great, but the more important accomplishment for value-stream owners and improvement teams is to make sure that *missed* targets get the required attention when needed (rather than being put off until the end of the project round). To accomplish that, start with a solid and realistic plan for how progress will be communicated, problems reported, new resources assigned, and contributions recognized. Two specific elements of lean management that are key to such a plan are *reviews* and *checks*.

Reviews: Formal sessions where performance-to-plan for each project goal is reported out by various team members and support roles, and countermeasures are proposed if problems exist.

Checks: Informal sessions, often in the form of a walkthrough or standup meetings at a tracking center, that occur frequently, where performance-to-plan for more specific action plan items are reviewed individually and it's confirmed that countermeasures are in place to address any problems that have been previously identified.

Lean Data Collection

A secondary goal of a VSI project is to help you build capability for making improvements beyond this project. Central to every improvement effort is the ability to capture and share results. For everyone to become involved in the improvement process, each person must learn how to measure his or her own performance relative to expectations. However, be aware that improvement efforts can easily become stalled if collecting and verifying the results is too much work.

Some project areas may not be tracking anything and have little or no real collective understanding of how well they are performing on a regular basis. Other areas might have many different measures of performance. In these cases, the measures usually fall into two categories: (1) measures that are difficult/time-consuming to collect and/or (2) results that generate little actual problem solving. In healthcare organizations, many reports get generated with detailed measures of all types of performance.

Some people may look at these on a regular basis, but staff is rarely engaged to routinely problem solve when there are disappointing trends. Occasionally, catastrophic events create "crisis" situations, where focus teams are tasked with addressing a specific issue. But rarely are these reports used to engage people in continuous improvement—there are too many measures, the data are typically backward-looking, and there is no management infrastructure to support it.

As you measure the current conditions and the results of your changes, think about the measurement methods (make them simple and easy to use) as well as the way the results can be used for ongoing continuous improvement. And if your results need to be tracked on an ongoing basis, make sure that your data collection is sustainable.

Another way to look at reviews and checks is from the perspective of metrics/targets. Remember that your measures (with targets) answer the question, "How do you know?" Your reviews and checks must answer the following performance questions.

1. Are we on schedule? (Level 1, Plan execution)

"Are we on schedule?" should be answered during regular informal checks and formal reviews. The answer to the question is referred to as a measure of *execution to plan*. Answering the question and communicating the answer can be easier if you use a visual tool such as the project-plan tracking tool or master schedule (see *St. Luke's Master Schedule* on page 111, or download a blank master schedule template at *lean.org/ppj*).

The master schedule includes the project goals with space to indicate whether each goal is on track as originally planned and whether the scheduled progress review has taken place. Similar templates can be used to track progress on the action plans for each of the goals. Or you can develop a master schedule that allows you to track both goals and action items on the same form (see *St. Luke's Master Schedule with Goals* on page 113).

If you find that you are off schedule (and the reality is that most projects get off schedule at some point), the next chapter of this guide will introduce you to the PDCA problem-solving method for identifying root causes and initiating problem solving to help you deal with what you learn.

2. Are we doing what we said we would do? (Level 1, Plan execution)

Answering this question is essential to making sense out of the process and value stream results you achieve. The focus is on the *means* the team has agreed to trial (the change). If results *are not* going as expected, check to see that everyone followed the original plan and performed the experiments as designed.

If some people involved in an experiment follow the plan to the letter and others revert back to the way they normally do things—because they didn't receive the directions, understand the directions, see the importance, or don't now how to problem solve when things don't go as expected—you will end up with results that won't really answer your questions about the impact of your experiment. And if the results are going as expected, check to make sure that the people involved didn't modify the original plan to get the results you hoped to achieve before the team was able to assess the impact of the original plan.

St. Luke's Master Schedule

Project: ED treat and release value stream

Process owner: Allen

Value-stream owner: Janet

Project champion: Natalie

Project Date: 06/01/2012 – 09/15/2012

Objective: Decrease length of stay for treatment and release to 2 hours

Decrease readmission by 50%

Project Review Date 1) July 1, 2012 Status ☐ 2) Aug. 1, 2012 Status ☐ Status ☐ **Final:** Sept. 15, 2012 Status ☐

Goals	Target	Responsible	Timeline						Support	Review
			June	July	Aug.	Sept.				
1. Standardizing D/C instruction	• Reduce readmissions by 50% • Trial complete Aug. 15	Allen							Allen	
2. Enhance triage role to include acuity, standard orders, and miniregistration	• MD/RN protocols in use on all shifts by Aug. 15	Sam							John	
3. Create SLAs with clinical support functions	• 2 SLAs by Aug. 30 • X-ray reports in 30 min	John							Jack	
4. Standardize and move registration after rooming to take advantage of waiting time in exam rooms	• Reduce door-to-doc time by 10 min by Aug. 15 • Increase satisfaction by 2% by Aug. 15	Pete							John	

Reviews

Signature Block	
Project Lead	
Project Owner	
Project Sponsor	
Function Executive	Ellen

Time Line Legend

Time Line ──	
Review ◇	Fill in when performed ◆
Planned start/end line ☐	Actual start/end time ■

Management to the Plan Evaluation Scale

◉ Implementation complete Impact confirmed

⊘ Implementation complete Impact unknown

◯ Implementation complete Impact insufficient

△ Implementation incomplete No impact

3. If we are doing what we said we would do the way we said we would do it, are we having the impact we expect to achieve on process performance?
(Level 2, Process performance)

Answering this question will take you back to your future-state metrics and possibly to your goal statements. The focus is on outcomes or impact at the process level. On your future-state map you estimated your new P/T and L/T (LOS) for each process or chunk, based on the improvements you expect to see if the changes you propose are executed successfully. In your goal statements, you also may have estimated a change in results for a process or chunk. For example, if you proposed to combine registration and triage in an ED project, as did St. Luke's, you may be looking to reduce the P/T and L/T for the first step or chunk in the process.

4. If we are doing what we said we would do the way we said we would do it, are we having the impact we expect to achieve for the performance of the entire value stream? (Level 3, Value-stream performance)

Answering this question will take you back to your overall project objective and the impact you hope to have on your value-stream performance. Here you are working off the assumption that improved performance of in-process metrics will lead to improved value-stream performance as well—for example, reducing the total LOS and, perhaps, improving patient satisfaction.

In both cases the results are *outcome measures*. Remember, outcome measures refer to factors like total LOS, patient satisfaction, patient safety (e.g., pressure ulcers), patients leaving without being seen, patients leaving against medical advice, and unplanned readmissions to the hospital within 48 hours. Also remember that although you want to monitor your value-stream metrics on a regular basis (e.g., monthly), it may take several rounds of improvement before you see impact to the entire value stream (see *Levels of Tracking* on page 114).

In a review or check, you are trying to determine if actual performance is going according to plan. If so, what is being done to "sustain" what you have accomplished? If not, what is being done to "close the gap?" Status reports and meetings tend to be one-way communications, limiting both learning and problem solving. Unlike a status report, each check or review should encourage goal owners and action-item owners to question if and how problems are being surfaced as well as what is being done to solve them. Individuals working on goals and action items should discuss progress, not just indicate status.

St. Luke's Master Schedule with Goals

Date: 05/15/2012
Project Owner: Allen
VS Owner: James

Master Schedule with Action Plan (1 Goal)

Value-Stream Goals: Reduce LOS to less than 2 hours, with no impact on satisfaction

Review frequency: 30 days
Process: ED treat and release
Area: St. Luke's ED

Value-stream goal	Action	Action target	Weekly Schedule	Action owner	Objective evaluation	Comments
Develop standardized discharge instructions in order to reduce readmissions	1. Select team from ED that will be invloved in developing new discharge instructions	June 5	06/01	Allen	■	Complete
	2. Establish %CA baseline for discharge instructions	June 15	06/15	Allen	■	Complete
	3. Team reviews existing documents and procedures for discharge	June 15	06/15	Mary	■	Complete
	4. Team identifies problems in existing procedures	June 20	06/15	Jen	■	Complete
Reduce readmissions by 50% by Aug. 15 Goal Owner: Allen	5. Develop standardized discharge documents for a trial	July 1	06/29	Allen	(light)	Limited resources to train staff on standardized procedure for trial
	6. Develop a measuring system to evaluate the trial	July 15	07/13	Mary	■	Communication area and metrics agreed to and collected for trials
	7. Conduct a trial over an agreed to timeframe	Aug. 5	08/03	Allen		
	8. Evaluate results and implement or do a retrial	Aug. 15	08/10	Allen		
Support: Pete						

Weekly Schedule column headers: 06/01, 06/08, 06/15, 06/22, 06/29, 07/06, 07/13, 07/20, 07/27, 08/03, 08/10, 08/17, 08/24, 08/31, 09/07, 09/14

A blank master schedule with goals template is available at *lean.org/ppj*

So for each of the performance levels described, the individual responsible should answer these questions:

- What is your planned performance?
- What is your actual performance?
- How are you surfacing problems?
- What problems have you encountered?
- What have you done/are doing to get back on track?

Formal reviews typically cover all three levels of performance as described previously—performance to plan (on schedule and doing what we said), and outputs and outcomes for in-process metrics and the entire value stream. (*You will learn more about formal reviews in Chapter 8.*)

Levels of Tracking: Plan Execution, Process Performance, and Value-Stream Performance

Level 1:
Execution to
schedule and plan

Level 2:
Value-stream
improvements
at process level

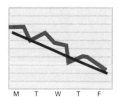

Patient door-to-doc times

Level 3:
Performance
improvement at
value-stream level

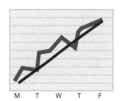

Number of patients discharged
in less than 2 hours

In an informal check, the dialogue may occur right where the work is done and address only the process (process improvements and in-process metrics). Informal checks typically last only 10 to 20 minutes and serve the following purposes:

- Verify that work on goals or actions is proceeding as planned.

- Verify that countermeasures are working as intended to address any problems that have been previously identified.

- Surface new problems and determine who will be responsible for identifying what actions need to be taken next. (Actual analysis of the problems and development of countermeasures may occur during the check or may be scheduled for a later time, sometimes after some additional facts have been collected.)

Checks typically do not involve formal reports in written form, and often are led by different members of the team. Typically, the value-stream owner checks progress on meeting the project goals with the goal owner and staff providing support. Goal owners check progress on action steps. And action owners check progress on the work being done to complete action steps.

Formal reviews should be scheduled to report progress at each major project milestone, typically at 30-day intervals for each round of implementing changes. Depending on your management plan, you may have two levels of review: one for goal owners to report progress to the process owner and a second one for the process owner and goal owners to report overall progress to the leadership team. (If resources are available, include improvement team members in the reviews as well.) Formal reports typically include handout material to supplement what appears on the project tracking center (*see page 117*).

Checks and Roles

Problem location	Problem-solving leader	Problem owner	Problem-solving participant
Goal	Value-stream owner	Goal owner	Goal support (including action owners)
Action step	Goal owner	Action owner	Action-step support
Action step	Action owner	Action-step support	Other stakeholders

Reviews are led by the value-stream owner, who should advise goal owners to come prepared to present a formal progress report that includes the following information for each goal and related action plan:

- Planned vs. actual: What should have been done by now, and what has actually been done.

- What progress has been achieved in making the planned change, and what have been the results and/or impact?

- What problems have been encountered, and how have they been/are they going to be addressed?

- What has been learned, and how will it be used?

Now that you understand the purpose of reviews and checks, you can determine who is going to conduct them and how often they need to be conducted. In a 90-day improvement cycle, the lean champion and other leadership team members, including the value-stream owner, should generally conduct formal reviews with the improvement team (or at least the goal owners) on a monthly basis. The process owner and lean facilitator should conduct their own formal reviews with key improvement team members (such as the goal owners) on a more frequent basis. All of the core team should plan some routine checks, typically on at least a weekly basis if not daily.

Since you are learning how to conduct reviews and checks while you are implementing changes, experiment with a few different methods for conducting the review to determine what works best for your organization.

Socializing Your Measures and Data Collection Plan

Socialize your data collection measures and plan to the rest of the staff, explaining the importance of collecting the data, how the data will be used, and what kind of support you need from them. Rallying support for data collection is easier if people can see that an "owner" is going to take the data and use it to move the organization to an "agreed to" goal and a valid target condition. It also gives frontline staff an opportunity to identify problems with the plan and generate some additional ideas to make the data collection simple, unobtrusive, and meaningful to everyone involved.

Make Progress Visible

While PDCA is at the heart of successful change and improvement, it's not the only lean ingredient necessary for success. You cannot correct your course if you cannot see how you have done so far. Visually tracking an improvement effort and its progress is just as important as using visual indicators and visual standards to spot problems at specific work areas or work procedures.

There are many ways to make your progress visible and to spot problems as they occur. One technique is to organize a single area where all the action can be seen at a glance— that is, a value-stream improvement tracking center or dashboard. The tracking center is a wall or a board (see *St. Luke's Value-Stream Tracking Center* below) positioned near the people who do the work in the value stream (or near the process owner) where you can post maps, plans, what you are measuring, and accomplishments. The center is where everyone can see immediately whether the project is on track.

St. Luke's Value-Stream Tracking Center

Current-State Value-Stream Map

Future-State Value-Stream Map

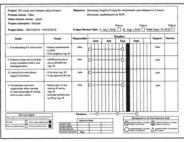

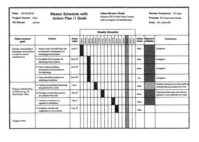

Master Schedule

Goals + Action Plan

In-process Measures

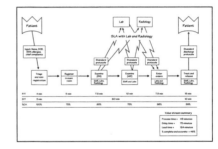

% readmit

%CA Lab/Rad

%OT Lab/Rad

Outcome Measures

Countermeasures

LOS

LWBS

This also is an opportune time to update your future-state map, adding information at the bottom of the map to indicate your plan for checks and reviews (see *St. Luke's Future-State Map with Checks and Reviews* on page 119).

Changing Role of Value-Stream Owner or Project Owner

As the project shifts from planning to doing, the role of the value-stream owner or project owner (depending on the scope of the project) changes to include some new responsibilities. These include:

• Maintaining a regular cadence of checks and reviews (See *St. Luke's Regular Check Points—Manage and Learn* below),

• Personally going to see what's happening as the plan is executed and hearing directly from the staff involved in the experiments,

• Leading problem solving when execution and experiments do not go as planned,

• Communicating and managing the relationship with the rest of the organization, done in coordination with the lean sponsor.

St. Luke's Regular Check Points—Manage and Learn

Radiology technologists track and check hourly

Daily plan for monitoring reported results				
Time	**# Planned**	**# Actual**	**Gap**	**Reason**
8–9 am				
9–10 am				
10–11 am				
11–12 pm				
Summary				
1–2 pm				
2–3 pm				
4–5 pm				
Summary				

Manager checks and reviews weekly

M T W T F

Supervisor checks and questions twice daily

St. Luke's Future-State Map with Checks and Reviews

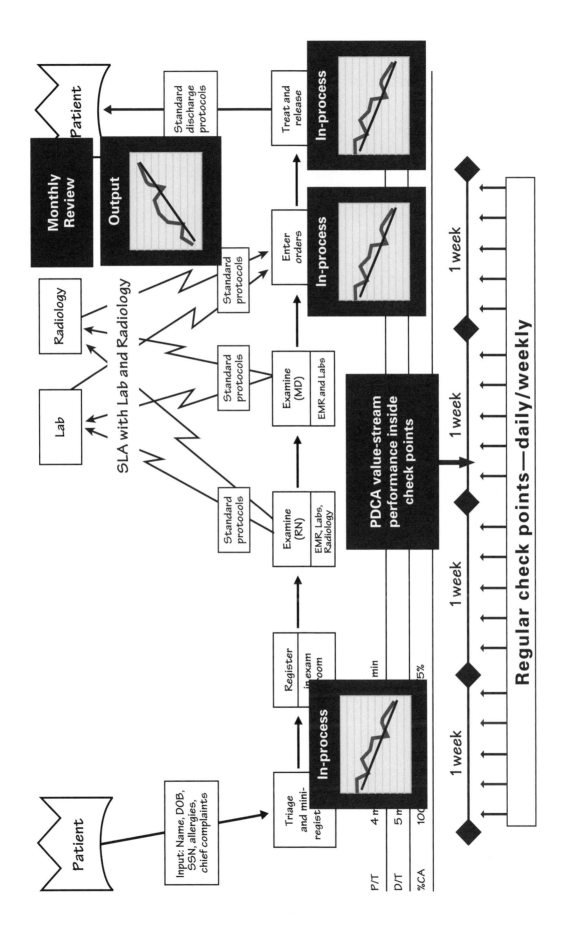

Standardized Work for Leaders

Both reviews and checks can be built into a standard routine, often referred to as leader standard or standardized work. Leader standardized work is both the standardized work for performing checks and reviews (the how) and the routine that a leader goes through to check on the value-stream performance under his or her responsibility (the when and where) to see how team members are progressing on the things they are trying to do and improve and what things out of their scope are adversely affecting what they are trying to do.

For example, a value-stream owner, such as a manager of the administrative department with ownership of the patient registration process, will conduct a daily walkthrough to ensure that the people working in the process are on pace to meet the daily requirements. On this walkthrough, the manager makes several stops to verify that the teams are tracking their performance, logging problems, and taking containment actions when appropriate. The manager asks questions when there are no problems (because no problem is a problem) and ensures that the team members are not simply building permanent workarounds if they repeatedly confront a problem. During the walk and through conversations, the manager may recognize that any recurring problems are due to the performance of related areas (not part of the improvement project) or to practices and policies in the organization as a whole; these are issues the manager needs to take the lead on addressing.

Ideally, the value-stream owner will schedule a permanent time on his or her calendar for this activity as well as a standard route for each walkthrough. The value-stream owner will have a checklist or some other visual aid that helps ensure consistency and that all the right things are checked. The owner should also have a standard approach for addressing the issues/problems that arise on the walkthrough, and engage the staff in PDCA problem solving—not solving the problem, even when he or she is certain of a solution.

Chapter 7
Keeping Your Improvement Project on Track

This chapter will help you and your team:

• Conduct a formal review to identify performance to plan, assess impact, and maximize learning.

• Make adjustments (run additional experiments to address emerging problems/issues).

• Learn lean problem-solving methods for checks and reviews.

• Establish three roles for those involved in checks and reviews.

Chapter 7
Keeping Your Improvement Project on Track

How Are You Doing?

During the first *do* phase (i.e., within the first 60–120 days) of your future-state plan, when you began to make changes and first conducted initial checks and review, you likely encountered some problems: Action plans ran behind or ahead of schedule. Experiments did not produce the results you expected. Experiments produced results but they also had unintended consequences. Changes did not affect your process outcomes—for specific chunks or for the whole value stream—as you anticipated.

Problems are typical. In fact, your project is right on schedule if you find yourself trying to deal with problems and the unexpected. You are beginning to learn what it will take to implement countermeasures that eventually achieve the future state.

Conducting a Formal Review

The formal review is a critical part of the implementation and experimentation phase of your improvement project. Typically, there are three or four formal reviews, scheduled approximately one month apart. The focus of a formal review is to assess planned vs. actual results for your project—planned progress on the plan, improvement in performance of the process, and planned impact of the changes compared to what is actually happening based on a thorough grasp of the situation. Reviews initiate the "check" of PDCA and will help to guide the development of additional countermeasures to get closer to your future-state goals.

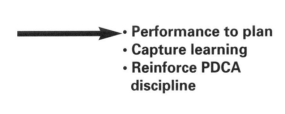

- Performance to plan
- Capture learning
- Reinforce PDCA discipline

Check

A typical agenda for a formal project review, including instructions for teams participating in the review, appears at right (*see page 125*). Expectations of the formal review are to:

- Make corrections to keep the plan on track toward achieving your goals,

- Create an opportunity for team members to learn how to address problems that emerged during implementation,

- Practice the discipline of PDCA,

- Capture learnings from the experiments.

Applying the Lean Approach to Problem Solving

No implementation ever goes as planned: you can't anticipate everything that will happen, and conditions change. Formal reviews help to identify what has happened and if conditions changed. The emergence of obstacles—as well as successes—means it's time for you and your team to implement problem solving to overcome obstacles and help you get back on track, to see what you can learn from obstacles and successes and apply elsewhere, and/or to modify your original plan. Here's how to apply the basic steps of problem solving to issues that emerge during your formal reviews.

1. Clearly define the problem in performance terms.

It's a given among lean practitioners that "a problem clearly defined is a problem half solved." This idea—develop a deep understanding of a problem before initiating action—runs counter to our cultural tendency to form quick judgments and offer up solutions. Too often these solutions do not match the real problem, in many cases because they are based on assumptions about the current condition that were never validated. In contrast, lean asks you to define the problem by looking at what is currently happening and comparing it to what should be happening. This means looking at whether the groups working on the specific goals have completed their assignments by the target dates (i.e., performance to plan). It also means looking at the experiments they are running to see if the results match their expectations.

Once your team has implemented the proposed changes, it means checking to see if you are sustaining the results and if you are having the impact you want on your in-process and value-stream outcomes (e.g., LOS, unplanned readmits, etc.). All of these actions constitute the check phase of the improvement cycle.

Agenda item and purpose	Instructions for teams	Time
Share accomplishments Team members reflect on what they've accomplished over the past 30 days.	• Teams sit in a circle or similar configuration so they can look at each other while they share successes they had during the past 30 days. This is a way for team members to appreciate each other's efforts.	1 hour
Performance analysis *Performance to plan:* Are we on schedule? Are we doing what we said we would do? *Performance of the process:* Are we meeting our expectations with respect to the value stream and process goals? *Impact of changes and experiments:* What are the specific outcomes of our experiments with respect to the expectations?	• Each team works together and analyzes the goals they have been working on, developing agreement on the analysis. Teams then make the analysis visible using whiteboard, flip chart, or white sheets. • Each team presents their analysis to the other teams.	1–2 hours
Execution analysis *What worked and what didn't?* Capture what actually happened. *What did we learn?* Capture what we learned about the value stream, our ability to make changes, and our ability to measure performance?	• Each team works together and analyzes the goals they have been working on, developing agreement on the analysis. Teams then make the analysis visible using whiteboard, flip chart, or white sheets. • Each team presents their analysis to the other teams.	1–2 hours
Develop countermeasures Brainstorm and select actions to overcome the difficulties from the analysis.	• Each team works together at identifying countermeasures for the problems listed above in each analysis.	1 hour
Next 30-day plan Develop/update the plan for the next 30 days including countermeasures and experiments.	• Each team creates and records the next 30-day plan, including both countermeasures and experiments. Plans must include a system for socializing the updated plan and identify specific actions, responsibility, and timing.	1 hour

Review or report to leadership
 	
Share accomplishments, learnings, and the next 30-day plan with leadership.
	• Each team provides a high-level report to the leadership team, which includes:
	  –Accomplishments (performance improvement and project execution),
	  –What was learned,
	  –Next 30-day plan.
		1 hour

For example, St. Luke's established the following goal:

Develop an SLA with Lab and Radiology to provide x-ray results within 30 minutes.

The purpose for this change was to reduce delay time associated with waiting for the test results. A check on the work group's progress indicated that the group had met with the Radiology team to discuss the need for an SLA and collected some baseline data, which revealed that response times were in excess of one hour more than 65% of the time. Next the group developed the criteria and a measurement system to run a trial on the impact of adopting the SLA and then ran trials on two shifts on the same day. Baseline data indicated that response times had improved slightly on both shifts (average times of 59 and 58 minutes). As a result, the team determined that some additional changes would likely be needed if Radiology were to meet the SLA.

That is a *problem*—a gap between where things are and where they are supposed to be. St. Luke's can quantify this gap in performance terms: *What should be happening is that the time for reporting results should be 30 minutes, and it currently is 58–59 minutes even with the SLA.*

2. Determine where in the work there are problems that contribute to the performance issue.

This step distinguishes problem solving based on facts vs. on assumptions and conclusions. For example, with no additional information, St. Luke's could conclude that the problem might be related to a lack of resources (e.g., not enough Radiology rooms or not enough technologists to staff the existing rooms). Instead, the goal owner and two workgroup members from the ED and Radiology decided to visit the gemba (Radiology) and talk to the workers on both shifts where the trials were run.

What they learned from their go-and-see experience was that:

• Sometimes not enough technologists were available to perform scans of ED patients.

• Technologists spent up to 15 minutes waiting for patient transport workers to bring patients to the equipment room.

• Orders for the scans were not entered until the patients arrived at the equipment room.

• Technologists also spent significant time prepping patients and prepping the room.

• Documenting information from the gemba can help make patterns clear.

3. Address (contain) the impact of the problem.

Addressing the impact of the problem means putting out the fire before you worry about fire prevention. In this case, containing the impact of the problem might involve repeated calls to Radiology to check on the status of imaging studies for individual patients. Making the calls is a *temporary measure* or *containment measure*—it works around the problem but does not address its direct cause. In this case, however, it might be appropriate to do the workaround to ensure that patients don't wait an excessive time for treatment, which is being delayed by the lack of imaging studies.

Other workarounds might be necessary to address a patient- or worker-safety issue. Unfortunately, in most environments, the problem solving stops right there. The workaround becomes the standard approach and the problem recurs. To keep that from happening, you and your team must delve deeper into the problem and identify the underlying cause(s).

4. Identify underlying cause(s) of the contributing problems.

Typically this step is done by going to the gemba, looking for the direct cause for what is happening, discussing the most likely causes, and validating causes by observation and data collection. Based on the trip to the gemba, the St. Luke's Radiology SLA workgroup observed the following direct causes:

- The number of techs available to do imaging studies for the ED varied, depending on whether one or more of them got called to the OR to do STAT scans.

- Patient transport workers were assigned to specific areas of the hospital and did not flex according to changes in the transport needs of different areas.

- Orders were not entered until patients arrived because the order entry was being performed by the Radiology technologist.

- Job duties for Radiology technologists included patient and room prep.

To identify most likely potential direct causes, you can use problem-analysis tools, such as fishbone diagrams, cloud diagrams, or problem-analysis trees (see cloud diagrams on page 128). These tools help you evaluate the most likely causes and their relative contribution to the problem. Further analysis will help you refine your understanding of the causes and set priorities for action.

Problem Situation

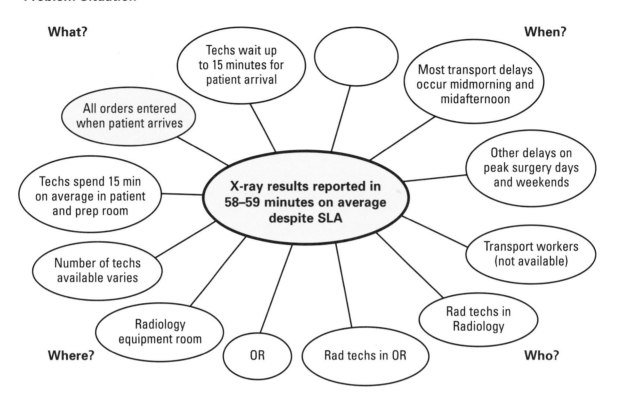

What?

Techs wait up to 15 minutes for patient arrival

All orders entered when patient arrives

Techs spend 15 min on average in patient and prep room

Number of techs available varies

Radiology equipment room

Where?

OR

Rad techs in OR

X-ray results reported in 58–59 minutes on average despite SLA

When?

Most transport delays occur midmorning and midafternoon

Other delays on peak surgery days and weekends

Transport workers (not available)

Rad techs in Radiology

Who?

Potential Cause Analysis

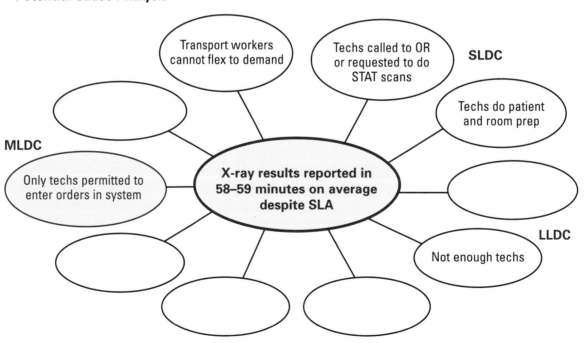

Transport workers cannot flex to demand

Techs called to OR or requested to do STAT scans

SLDC

Techs do patient and room prep

MLDC

Only techs permitted to enter orders in system

X-ray results reported in 58–59 minutes on average despite SLA

LLDC

Not enough techs

MLDC = Most likely direct cause   **SLDC** = Somewhat likely direct cause   **LLDC** = Least likely direct cause

We suggest you start with a cause that provides the biggest potential return on your investment of time and effort or that which provides the best chance for quick success. Regardless of whether you use such tools, you may want to take another trip to the gemba to validate the potential causes.

The next step is to identify underlying causes, which will help you to prevent fires rather than just extinguish them. By identifying the underlying causes down to the root causes, you can reduce the likelihood that a given problem will recur. By identifying the root cause for a serious problem, such as a reportable event, you also may prevent future serious problems of a similar type because of what you have learned from addressing root cause for the initial event. As an example of the former, consider children with severe and poorly controlled asthma. Such children are frequent visitors to hospital EDs. You can provide the best possible care to an asthmatic child in the ED and send him home with the appropriate meds, inhalers, and clear instructions for his caregivers. But it's only by sending someone to visit the home, doing an environmental assessment, discovering mold that permeates the child's living space, and addressing that issue that your little patient will spend weeks or months free of acute episodes and readmissions.

Root-Cause Investigation with Cause

At St. Luke's, the workgroup's visit to the gemba and analysis of data confirmed that orders were not being entered until the patient arrived because the orders were being entered by the technologists. Root-cause analysis for the problem was as follows:

Orders were not entered until patients arrived because the Radiology technologists were entering the orders.

└→ **WHY are orders not entered until the patient arrives?**
Because management assumed that all tasks associated with performing imaging studies needed to be done by a Radiology technologist.
therefore ⟩

└→ **WHY did management assume technologists were required for all tasks?**
Because a skills analysis was never done to see if there was nonskilled work associated with performing imaging studies that could be done by someone other than a Radiology technologist.
therefore ⟩

└→ **WHY weren't nonskilled work opportunities explored?**
Because historically the hospital had always had sufficient Radiology technologists to meet the demand.

There are many different ways to do root-cause analysis. The root-cause approach used at many lean organizations consists of selecting the most likely underlying causes (one level at a time), asking and answering "Why?" to get to each subsequent level, then investigating to find and confirm the next level of underlying cause until you reach the root cause. The root cause is the cause that set the chain of cause-effect links in motion, leading to the initial effect—the problem that you defined as the starting point for your cause investigation.

To confirm that you have developed a sound cause-effect chain, start at the end of the sequence and work your way backward, leaving out "because" and adding "therefore" at the end of each statement. For the chain above, the sequence would begin like this:

> *The hospital historically had sufficient Radiology technologists to meet demand. Therefore, no skill analysis was performed for the job to identify tasks that could be performed by someone other than a technologist. Therefore, management assumed that all tasks associated with imaging studies needed to be done by a Radiology technologist.*

If you can demonstrate a sound cause-effect chain by following the sequence in reverse, you are ready to begin experimenting to confirm true cause. That means you begin to implement countermeasures for each cause and you'll know that you've reached the true root cause when the entire cause-effect chain is broken and the problem goes away.

Five Whys

The lean technique of exploring problems by repeatedly asking "Why?"—often referred to as the "Five Whys"—is effective, but it can be viewed as annoying or intrusive if not done in a context whereby all involved in the conversation understand its use as a problem-solving tool. The St. Luke's example shows a single answer to the question "Why?" but in reality each "Why?" may have multiple answers, each of which needs to be answered with another "Why?" in its own causal chain.

5. Develop/plan countermeasures to the causes.

By the time you do this level of analysis, the countermeasures that need to be developed are often pretty obvious. Close to the surface level of cause, it's clear that management (e.g., HR) might need to be approached about the need to review the work of the Radiology technologists, followed by a job analysis for the position and perhaps reallocation of tasks requiring less skill.

At a more fundamental level, leadership needs to consider that all positions might be revisited to look for ways to reallocate duties that do not require specific licensure, certification, or highly technical skills. (This countermeasure refers to a type of organizational learning that goes well beyond the specific problem of technologists entering orders for imaging studies.)

6. Implement and test the countermeasures.

Once you develop countermeasures for any problems that have surfaced, document them in writing and post them at your tracking center. To ensure follow through, countermeasure documentation should include the problem to be addressed, the corresponding countermeasure, the target (for quality and/or for completion), the person responsible for seeing that the countermeasure is implemented and tested to see if it solves the problem, and any support required. Most countermeasure sheets also include a review date, the person who will do the review, and a place for the reviewer's initials once the review is completed.

Problem Countermeasures					
Problem	Cause	Countermeasure	Responsible	Target date	Review date

The Need to Act Regardless of Outcomes

No plan ever gets executed exactly as written, which means your future-state changes will be modified or replaced at some point—consider your plan a working document. When you recognize that an experiment has yielded an unexpected result, you need to act. If your experiment produces an outcome that meets or exceeds your targets and you can replicate the results, your action might be to determine how to spread this learning to other situations. Depending on the context and the experiment, this spreading might be as straightforward as moving a supply cabinet, or as complex as introducing a new protocol across all ED clinical staff. In either case, you are performing the "A" of smaller PDCA cycles in the *do* phase of your project, which leads you to add or modify your improvement plan.

If you run an experiment and the results fall short of your expectations, your *act* will be to analyze the experiment to determine the cause of the shortfall and put additional countermeasures in place to address this cause. Each new countermeasure should adhere to lean principles. To be sure this is the case, evaluate each new countermeasure according to the following lean rules:

1. All work should be specified as to content, sequence, timing, and outcome.

2. Every customer-supplier connection must be direct, and there must be an unambiguous, yes-or-no way to send requests and receive responses.

3. The pathway for creating and/or delivering each service or product must be simple and direct.

4. Any improvement must be made in accordance with the scientific method, at the lowest possible level in the organization, and with the support of a teacher (i.e., someone who is more experienced at PDCA problem solving) as needed.[3]

These four lean rules strive to eliminate "discretionary" or "judgment-based" systems for *managing* work but not necessarily for performing the work itself where judgment is required. When there is ambiguity around who does what, when something should be done, and who must decide how it's done, there also is ambiguity around what constitutes a problem. This is particularly disruptive to the flow of work. Judgment-based systems for managing the work, in which rules change at someone's discretion, should be replaced by reflexive systems that are based on agreed-to protocols (see *Reflexive vs. Cognitive Systems* on page 133).

---

3. Adapted from Spear & Bowen, "Decoding the DNA of the Toyota Production System, *Harvard Business Review*, September 10, 1999. "Teacher" in this context can be viewed as an internal or external lean consultant.

Reflexive vs. Cognitive Systems

Reflexive systems are the backbone of a lean value stream and consist of clearly defined rules that govern how all the steps in the process are supposed to work. With reflexive systems, work will usually move according to plan unless there is a problem.

In contrast, cognitive systems are expert-based and rely on expert people or software having access to the work-status information. These cognitive systems rely on judgment or discretion to then "calculate" the optimal schedules or priority to make the best use of resources. Because a cognitive system relies on an expert, only the expert can determine if there is a problem. The expert then must convince others that a problem is real.

Cognitive systems abound in healthcare settings. For example, any time a doctor or nurse has to remember to go back and check on something (like lab results) or someone (like the status of a patient), that is a cognitive system. Many times additional workarounds are put in place to remind the individual or alert them when they have forgotten something. These workarounds often take the form of additional interruptions (e.g., the person who forgot is interrupted with a page or a phone call).

In contrast, a reflexive system based on rules has flags or trip-wires built in. The signal is given in the normal course of work, or there is a preset time or routine when the person looks for the signal. When there is a problem with the flow of work, it is clearly visible to all stakeholders without the use of interruptions. Moreover, when there is an occurrence where the prescribed notification method cannot take place, the disruption in flow is clearly visible to everyone, so there is no question about a need for action to address the problem.

At St. Luke's, the initial selected countermeasure was a job analysis that revealed that someone other than the Radiology technologist could be trained to enter orders correctly. Training manuals were developed, and the ED clerks were trained to enter the orders, which they were able to do with 72.3% accuracy within one week of being trained. And by moving order entry to the clerks, the SLA workgroup was able to remove 5 to 7 minutes from the delay time for imaging studies. Recognizing that the work was not finished (there was still a gap of 24 to 21 minutes between the improved performance and the SLA goal), the group continued to work on the accuracy of the ED clerk order entries. It also revisited the initial list of likely direct causes, performed a separate root-cause analysis on each, and initiated a related project focused on eliminating other nontechnical work performed by the Radiology technologists.

Problem-Solving Roles

In the previous section of this chapter, you learned what to do to address problems related to your improvement effort. In this section you will learn how to lead problem solving during that effort, specifically during checks and reviews. In lean organizations, managers and supervisors have equal responsibility for improving work *and* for developing the problem-solving abilities of the people who report to them.

Before learning about lean roles to accomplish that, review the following mechanics for efficiently conducting an informal check and/or formal reviews:

- Select a consistent time and date for reviews (e.g., fourth Thursday of the month at 10 a.m.).

- Hold the review at the tracking board.

- Have participants stand during the meeting to keep them alert.

- Ask each goal owner to present his or her "performance to plan."

- If performance is not to plan, lead the goal owner in problem solving to identify the most likely causes. Assign the goal owner to confirm root causes and return with an agreed "countermeasure" to get back on plan or in some cases propose a modification to the plan.

- Spend less time reviewing goals that are going to plan and the bulk of the time reviewing those that are not going well (but don't ignore things that go well!).

- Make sure to allow time for goal owners who reported problems at the previous session to report on the countermeasures they have implemented.

Three major roles are involved in reviews, with each having unique responsibilities for keeping the dialogue constructive during the review:

1. Problem owner

The problem owner (e.g., a goal owner or action-item owner) has responsibility for seeing that problems get solved. However, that doesn't mean the owner is necessarily doing all the work. At reviews, the owner's role is to present what has been done and the results that have been achieved. The owner also presents the problems the team has encountered (and perhaps some of their analysis and their proposed countermeasures). The owner can help others play their roles effectively by presenting problems, new/revised targets, complete analyses, and, if appropriate, multiple options for countermeasures in a way that is clear, concise, and direct.

The PO also can get the group's report off to a good start by repeating the pertinent goal statement (change plus purpose and targets) to provide a framework for the report. If the team has identified barriers or obstacles that require help from superiors, the review is the venue for the PO to ask for assistance.

2. Problem-solving leader

The problem-solving leader, typically the process owner, is probably the most critical role in a review. The leader typically determines how productive the session is, in part by creating and maintaining an environment in which all present understand that they are expected to participate in the dialogue as equals regardless of their professional title or their position on the organizational chart. The leader can make the session more productive by reminding everyone at the beginning of the review of the purpose for the problem solving (i.e., the overall project objective and the expected benefits if the project succeeds).

The leader is responsible for achieving the purpose of the problem-solving effort but not for the effort itself. It is often easy for a leader to unintentionally take away responsibility from the owner and other participants and assume ownership of problems. The leader also can unintentionally influence the style of the dialogue. For that reason the leader must consciously work to keep the dialogue constructive, such as:

- Asking for clarification or justification in a way that does not put the other parties on the defensive,

- Modeling appropriate behavior for others in the group,

- Suggesting potential approaches to the problem in a way that does not assume control.

Clarifying questions are designed to solicit additional information during the review. They typically begin with "what" and "how":

- What did you do?

- What have you tried?

- What was done?

- How was/is it done?

- What were the results?

- How did it go?

- What impact did you observe?

- How big was the change?

Such clarifying questions, particularly if they are delivered in a manner that communicates, "I'm genuinely interested and I want to understand," keep the problem owner talking and help the leader and other participants understand the situation.

Asking for justification can be a more delicate task. When a superior asks a "Why?" question, it may sound as if an accusation or a negative judgment is being made. When that happens, dialog is likely to become defensive or actually shut down. If "Why?" questions are used, they should be directed only toward the process and only when the problem owner has initiated that type of analytical dialogue.[4]

As an alternative, the leader can frame a question as a request for supporting information without using the word "why," e.g., "What makes you think that? What evidence is there to support that view? How did the team arrive at that conclusion?" Again, such questions should encourage the respondent to anchor his or her response in facts: "What specifically did you see? Can you show us?"

Teams often struggle to identify an appropriate countermeasure or perhaps they jump too quickly to one without considering other alternatives. In such cases, the leader may use a third type of question, the probing query, e.g., "What do you think would happen if ...?"

---

4. Note that questions concerning why someone did not follow standardized work are acceptable because they are a form of "why didn't you follow the plan?" Standardized work is the planned work; analyzing why it was not followed can surface barriers to be addressed.

3. Problem-solving participants

Problem-solving participants have a strong vested interest in seeing the problem solved, but they must work with the problem owner to solve it. A participant might be formally listed on a goal or action step as a resource or simply be another team member or stakeholder. Because participants are participating in the actual experiments and implementation efforts, they often represent an important observational perspective, sometimes one that contradicts the perspective of the owner. In such cases, the participant needs to speak from his or her own direct observations, e.g., "That was not my experience. I had four nurses come to me last week looking for the forms."

In contrast, a participant response that begins with, "I don't think you're right ... I heard that...." is likely to shut down the dialogue or turn it into an argument. When presenting opinions, a participant should present the facts first, then the conclusions drawn from them. Moreover, whenever participants can share their assumptions when presenting opinions, it helps others understand how he or she arrived at a given conclusion, e.g., "Four nurses came to me looking for the forms. I assume they had been through the training. That's why I think the location of the forms needs to be reconsidered." Presenting the observable facts, the assumptions based on the facts, and then the conclusions drawn from the assumptions is, in fact, a practice that should be used by all those present at the review.

At any review or check, participants may find themselves in one or more of the above roles. Recognizing their role(s) and using the appropriate dialogue will enable the attendees to keep the session productive. Remember, these sessions are not simply to report status. Status is available on the tracking center at any time. Reviews and checks are designed to ensure that problems are being solved, results shared, and problem solving continues. To achieve those ends, reviews and checks must be structured for *problem-solving dialogue*, which leads to action/adjustments made during the session itself or in followup sessions scheduled shortly thereafter.

Keep Checks and Reviews Moving Along

As teams begin to conduct reivews and checks, it's not uncommon for a 30-minute standup meeting to drag. That generally happens because the participants are starting to lapse into conversation, rather than sticking to a strict agenda of PDCA. A tip for addressing this issue is to ask, "What topic are we trying to address, e.g., analyze the problem, look for root cause, select countermeasures, etc.?" If you can get all the participants addressing the same topic, the group can usually move ahead more efficiently.

Chapter 8
Moving Forward—From Projects and Events to Consistent Practice

This chapter will help you and your team:

- Conduct an end-of-project review and reflection.

- Learn how to stabilize the process and sustain improvements.

- Continue to solve problems.

- Address organizational and cultural barriers to continuous improvement.

- Share your learnings.

- Seize the next opportunity for improvement and continue to solve problems.

Chapter 8
Moving Forward—From Projects and Events to Consistent Practice

Project Reflection and Review

The end of your first round of value-stream improvement is a good time to step back and reflect on your project—what's been done, what still needs to be done, and what it means for the value stream you targeted for improvement and for your entire organization. The end-of-project review and reflection brings your PDCA cycle of improvement full circle, and prepares you to start the PDCA cycle over again.

As you learned in Chapters 7 and 8, reviews during a project enable a team to assess execution of the plan (on schedule and doing what was planned) and progress toward outcomes (in-process performance and value-stream performance). The aim is to identify gaps between planned vs. actual and address them through problem solving and rapid learning experiments. As a result of reviews, you identified and solved a lot of problems on your way to solving your original problem or making your intended change.

In contrast, the end-of-project review and reflection is intended for all involved to pull back to a higher and broader view in order to assess performance to purpose for the project as a whole, and to reflect on what was learned that can be used when deciding subsequent actions. Options for next actions depend on comparison of actual performance and outcomes to the original stated purpose (*see pages 140–141*).

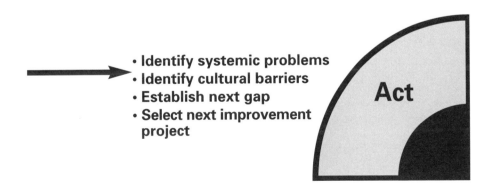

- **Identify systemic problems**
- **Identify cultural barriers**
- **Establish next gap**
- **Select next improvement project**

Act

Continue to Solve Problems

During the first 60–120 days of your project you ran small and large experiments and made changes that produced results in your designated value stream. Some targets were achieved or exceeded while other targets remain. You most likely surfaced new problems during this effort: some will get addressed with countermeasures and others will linger.

Once you begin to think about transitioning from "the project" to incorporating PDCA into your normal, everyday routines, take a few minutes to go back to the original problem you were trying to solve and to your future-state map. What was your problem statement? Is the problem still relevant? Have you achieved what you set out to accomplish in your project? What items or problems remain from your first 60–120 days and/or from your future-state map?

Once you answer those questions, make a choice:

1. Group the unmet targets and unfinished future-state work into a second 60–120 day project (complete with goals and action plans), or

2. Address the unmet targets and unfinished work as a series of individual projects that you tackle as continuous-improvement (CI) activities.

Project Reflections

For the project	1. What did you accomplish? (Review) How did you accomplish it? (Reflect)
	2. What was not done or accomplished? (Review) Why? (Reflect)
	3. Next steps on your project: 　• What do you need to complete or accomplish? How? (Continue problem-solving) 　• What do you need to capture and make part of normal practice? How? (Sustain)
	4. What conditions outside the value stream and the scope of the project hindered your efforts? How? (Moving Forward)
	5. What opportunities do you see to further improve performance? How? (Moving Forward)
For the team	1. What have you learned? (Reflect)
	2. Where can you apply what you've learned? (Moving Forward)

If you choose No. 1, you will need to consult with leadership to gain commitment (in particular a commitment of staff time) for an additional project. If you choose No. 2, you will need to spend some time thinking about whether there is a logical sequence or critical pathway that would help you sequence the individual CI projects.

Options for Next Actions

Performance and outcomes to purpose	Next actions
Implementation is not completed, change(s) are not fully implemented, expected outcomes are not achieved, and/or additional problems remain after implementation.	Reflect on why and *continue problem solving.*
Implementation completed as planned, changes made, outcomes achieved, and problems that arose are resolved.	Reflect on how this occurred, and work on ways to *sustain the improvements.* This includes *sharing changes and practices* that worked and *looking for other applications for improvements* that have increased capability and improved performance.
Planned changes have been made, the process stabilized, and measures in place to assure the improvements are maintained and consistent performance is sustained	Think of how to *create the process capability to move to the next level of performance and look for opportunities* to do it though further problem solving and additional improvement initiatives. This includes *looking at barriers to change and improvements* that were encountered but were part of the larger operational, organizational, or cultural context and beyond the scope of the project team to address. For example, systems that reward individual success rather than the success of teams. If these obstacles remain they will hinder further efforts at problem solving and continuous improvement by the value streams.

St. Luke's End-of-Project Review and Reflection

The team involved with St. Luke's ED treat-and-release value stream reviewed achievements over the previous months compared to their planned targets and chose the following paths forward.

End-of-Project Review and Reflection

Problem statement: ED faces long waits for low-acuity patients, high staff turnover, and potential loss of market share to other hospitals in the region.

Project objective: Reduce the average LOS for treat-and-release patients to 2 hours within 12 months—with no deterioration in customer or staff satisfaction or clinical outcomes and no increase in treatment costs.

Problems	Goals	Targets	Actual	End-of-project choices
Quality issues with discharge instructions	Standardize D/C instructions in order to decrease the % of readmissions	• Reduce readmissions by 50% • Trial complete by Aug. 15	• 30% • Aug. 25	• Goal owner to get original team back together to problem solve and implement countermeasures, possibly leading to new project on this issue
Standing orders used only 35% of the time	Enhance triage role to include acuity, standard orders, and miniregistration in order to start treatment sooner for certain protocols	• MD/RN protocols established by June 1 • Triage staff fully trained by June 30 • Evidence of protocols in use on all shifts by Aug. 15	• Established July 1 • Established July 30 • 80% compliance after 2-month random audit	• N/A • N/A • Goal owner to get original team back together to problem solve and implement countermeasures
Excess wait time for Lab and Radiology	Create SLAs with clinical support functions	• Reports for x-rays in less than 30 minutes • SLAs in use by Aug. 30	• 29-min average for 90% • Audits in Sept. and Oct. showed 95% compliance	• (ED) Goal closed • Monitor weekly • New project for general Radiology value-stream with patient transport
Patients have long delays in waiting area	Standardize and move registration after rooming to take advantage of patient wait times in exam rooms	• Reduce door-to-doc time by 10 minutes by Aug. 15 • Increase patient satisfaction by 2% by Aug. 15	• Reduced current door-to-doc time from 45 to 28 minutes • Patient satisfaction improved by 3%	• Monitor weekly • Review again during next patient-satisfaction survey

A blank project review and reflection template is available at *lean.org/ppj*

Make Continuous Improvement Standard Procedure

In implementing the system of measurements, checks, reviews, and countermeasures associated with your project, you established the essential elements of a management system for continuous improvement: a clear connection between the value stream and the customer, including what your customers really value, and responsibility for value-stream improvement (i.e., a value-stream owner), equipped with the right metrics and review/check methods to regularly monitor performance of the system.

Continuous improvement depends on consistent procedures and standard practices. Both problem solving and continuous improvement depend on standard-work procedures and work-performance standards that make clear where you should be and highlight both abnormalities to be addressed and opportunities to improve. Capturing best practices and making work procedures and standards visible will stabilize work processes that have been improved and create a foundation for further problem solving and continuous improvement.

Continuous improvement is as much about discipline as it is about creating a better way, and comes in two key forms:

- *Documenting and teaching work processes and procedures that have proven to produce targeted results*: Consistent effort to follow those processes and procedures will highlight the need for problem solving when they cannot be followed, and will reveal opportunities for improvement when they have delivered predictable results consistently.

- *Regularly followed practices to check status and look for and react to abnormal conditions*: Developing routine practices for looking for waste in work processes and bottlenecks in workflow is key to recognizing opportunities for improvement.

One way to promote the habit of continuous improvement is to institute leader standard work as was described in Chapter 7. Leader standard work helps your organization build CI into management's responsibilities—not just for supporting projects but for initiating CI as a regular practice. When leaders routinely go to see what is happening at the process level and ask why things are the way they are, it forces people to step outside their routines, escape the firefighting or workaround modes, and focus time and attention on systematic problem solving.

Address the Systemic and Cultural Barriers to Continuous Improvement

The end-of-project review and reflection also examines your improvement effort and outcomes in the context of the technical and social forces that surround the value stream and its processes:

Technical forces: Skill level of employees and leaders, capability of supporting systems, structure of the organization and its policies and practices, etc.

Social forces: culture of the organization, management environment, clarity of roles, character of relationships, etc.

Consider how forces influence success and the stability of the improvements that have been made. How did they affect efforts in the project, and how could they influence value-stream performance in the future? It helps to have a tool—e.g., a force-field diagram—to capture those forces, decide whether they function as drivers or barriers, and consider how to address or leverage them (see *St. Luke's Force-Field Diagram* on page 145). Drivers and barriers can be part of the social and cultural systems of your organization as well as your operating systems. Technical barriers can be analyzed through root-cause problem solving, but addressing these barriers with countermeasures will often require leveraging or addressing social forces as well.

Capitalize on Project Successes—Sharing the Learning

This guide has helped you focus on both the technical and social aspects of problem solving at each PDCA phase. If you solve the problems as you encounter them, or at least make significant progress, you have a story that should be shared.

When you think about telling this story, consider two different perspectives:

• The problem (both the problem you want to solve and the results you expect to achieve by solving it), and

• The process you use to solve it (the capability you want to build in the organization around problem solving).

Every organization ultimately defines its own destiny by its ability to solve problems over the long-term. For that reason, a value-stream improvement project is an exercise in building problem-solving skills while working on a real problem that your organization cares about. For example, if you work on a patient flow problem through the hospital, you will likely learn about the importance of making status visible and/or the causes of delays that prolong length of stay. You will also learn about handoffs between the functions that negatively or positively impact the patient. Consider how you can apply what you learned during the project to other problems. Where else in the organization might those tools be used to help improve the performance of a process? And how can you tell the story of your success?

St. Luke's Force-Field Diagram

The St. Luke's treat-and-release team identified failure to get broad and consistent engagement in activities of the actions teams as a force that contributed to delays in implementing planned changes. During the review and reflection, the question arose of how to get broader participation in subsequent efforts. The team created a force-field diagram that identified the forces recognized as barriers to engagement in the project and those that could be leveraged to increase participation. By doing so team members were able to identify actions they could take to increase the likelihood of greater involvement in future projects.

Increase and sustain engagement by ED staff in project-team activities

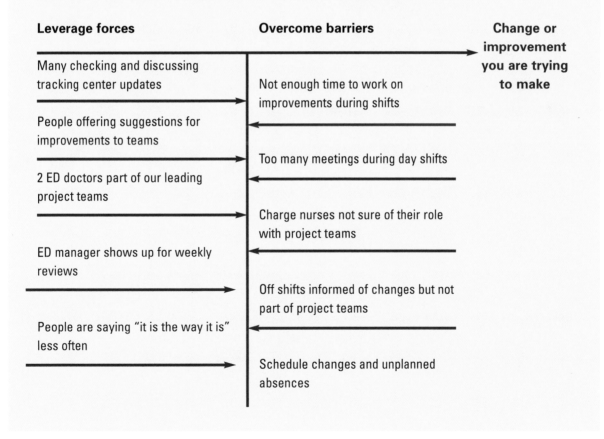

Leverage forces	Overcome barriers	Change or improvement you are trying to make
Many checking and discussing tracking center updates	Not enough time to work on improvements during shifts	
People offering suggestions for improvements to teams	Too many meetings during day shifts	
2 ED doctors part of our leading project teams	Charge nurses not sure of their role with project teams	
ED manager shows up for weekly reviews	Off shifts informed of changes but not part of project teams	
People are saying "it is the way it is" less often	Schedule changes and unplanned absences	

Seize the (Next) Opportunity, and the Next and the Next

As you consider moving forward at the end of a project, remember the approach you've taken and how it will apply elsewhere.

1. **Select and scope:** Identify a business need, define the problems, and provide a clear scope for the improvement effort.

2. **Map and plan:** Utilize value-stream mapping methods first to see what the end-to-end process or current-state value stream really looks like (not just a single step), and then identify performance gaps compared to the business need. Use mapping to create a vision for an improved future state and turn an abstract vision into tangible goals, targets, action steps, and metrics.

3. **Execute, check, and reflect:** Take action through experiments, measure the results, and solve the new problems (technical and social) that surface using disciplined root-cause techniques. Check and review performance regularly, implementing additional countermeasures, and make PDCA part of the regular routine.

As you complete each of the steps, make sure you socialize each draft product with the appropriate stakeholders and address their recommendations and concerns appropriately. And as you see progress, celebrate your successes and share what you've learned.

Seeing together with others creates alignment so that you can effectively make positive changes and create sustainable problem-solving habits. Within a portion of your organization, you have established an approach (scientific method), customer and purpose perspective (value stream, not "my work"), and culture (problem solving rather than workarounds and firefighting). Now you can you move beyond success in this particular value stream and make continuous improvement a regular part of the way you manage and operate throughout your organization.

Congratulations. You've reached the inflection point between "business as usual" and "systemic problem solving and improvement." Based on the experiences you have as you complete your project, the time is right to spread your success throughout your organization. Seize the moment!

Appendix: Value-Stream Improvement Roles

Role	Responsibilities
Lean champion	• Provides the link to leadership during project
	• Participates in scoping the project
	• Presents the project authorization (problem statement and value proposition) at project kickoff
	• Supports value-stream owner and lean facilitator
	• Regularly reviews project status through all phases of project
	• Acts as roadblock buster for implementation
	• Looks for opportunities (e.g., all-employee meetings) to reinforce standard communication messages regarding lean activities and improvement projects
	• Ensures accountability for completion of projects
	• Recognizes employees for successful project implementation
Lean facilitator	• Assists with preparation for workshops and socialization sessions
	• Facilitates workshops with the process owner
	• Facilitates briefings with leadership stakeholders
	• Helps participants thoroughly complete implementation plan
	• Assigned as lead coach for "kaizen bursts" (e.g., specific improvement activities) that are designated on the future-state map
Value-stream owner	• Invites and ensures appropriate participation from stakeholders
	• Manages implementation of the plan through scheduled reviews
	• Retains primary responsibility for overall value-stream performance
Improvement team	• Identifies how and how well the value-stream currently performs and documents that understanding in a current-state map
	• Creates a vision of how the value-stream would perform if problems were eliminated and documents that vision in a future-state map
	• Prioritizes problems to address in a 60-to-120-day improvement effort
	• Develops a plan to address the problems identified for the first round of improvements
	• Engages staff outside of the improvement team in running experiments and testing changes to improve the value stream
	• Participates in or provides updates on progress for scheduled reviews
	• Captures and shares project learning with other staff working in the value-stream and with the rest of the organization

Role	Responsibilities
Leadership panel (includes lean champion and perhaps value-stream owner)	• Selects the value stream for improvement, identifies the performance gap to be addressed, and ensures linkage to strategic priorities • Authorizes the project • Reviews progress on a regular basis • Identifies and addresses systemic problems (barriers) to progress • Ensures resources needed to complete the project • Addresses cross-departmental/functional conflicts that block progress
Steering committee	• Reviews value streams selected for improvement and ensures alignment with organizational priorities and resources • Addresses systemic problems that require intervention above the level of individual leadership panels • Leads effort to integrate results of projects into the management system • Identifies and plans structural changes required to support development of a problem-solving culture (e.g., HR, Finance and Accounting, etc.) • Identifies and plans changes required to move from functional management to value-stream management (including information technology)

Glossary of Lean Terms

General Lean Terms

Customer: The person(s), work unit, or functional area that use(s) what the value stream or process produces (i.e., the output).

Customer requirements: What the customer needs with regard to the output of the value stream or process, how many how quickly, how well, etc.

Flow: The movement of work through a value stream.

Lean: A set of concepts, principles, and tools used to create and deliver the most value from the customer's perspective while consuming the fewest resources and fully utilizing the knowledge and skills of the people performing the work.

Metrics: The measures used to observe or count specific items, activities, or resources to help determine how well a value stream is functioning and where problems occur. Typical value-stream metrics include process time, delay time, leadtime, length of stay, and percent complete and accurate. However, a group seeking to improve a process may choose to include other metrics such as sentinel events, full-time employees, and staff availability.

Output: The work product or result produced by a value stream or process.

Problem: The gap between the way things are now and the way they're supposed to be/you want them to be in the future.

Rework: Having to redo the work over again because it is not complete, not done correctly, or missing some important information.

Supplier: The person, work unit, or functional area that triggers the start of a value stream or process by sending an input (e.g., information, materials, a patient) to the process.

Supplier inputs: What the supplier sends to the first process that triggers the value stream to begin or what an upstream process or other supplier (e.g., the Lab) sends to a dowstream process to trigger the work in that process. The input is usually information, materials, or some combination of the two. In healthcare, patients also can be inputs. An example of a supplier input is when a patient is brought by EMS, along with specific information about their condition, to the emergency department. On value-stream maps, inputs are usually described in terms of volume (e.g., number of patients seen per shift or per day).

Value stream: All processes (and individual steps within processes), both value-creating and nonvalue-creating, required to complete a service or product from beginning to end.

Project Methodology

Action plans: Written statements of the action steps/project activities that need to be completed to achieve a project goal. Each action step includes an "owner," a target (timing and/or impact), and resources.

Elevator speech: A brief speech that explains what you are trying to do, why you are trying to do it, and engages the listener in supporting your project.

In-process measures/metrics: Measures or metrics that look at the function of some part of the value stream or process. The following are examples: the number of patients per shift who were not roomed immediately upon arrival or the number of blood samples drawn by ED staff that had to be discarded by the lab because of improper storage or delays in pickup. In-process measures can be used to gather baselines data and to see whether a specific intervention (an action plan) is having the impact you are looking for on some part of the value stream.

Outcome or output measures/metrics (also called summary statistics): Measures or metrics that look at the overall performance of a value-stream or process. For example, the ED's average leadtime or length of stay per patient is an outcome measure.

Performance-to-plan measures/metrics: Measures that look at how well an improvement plan is progressing according to the project schedule and desired impact.

Problem statement: A brief statement of the business, clinical, or customer-service issue that leadership has identified for improvement. The statement describes both the current situation (in objective, measurable terms) and the potential benefit of addressing it. The following is an example: Our surgical suites are currently in use only 40% of the available time, and we have a large backlog of people who need surgery. Increasing utilization (i.e., the number of surgeries performed) would decrease the wait time for our patients and significantly improve our annual revenue.

Project goals: Written statements that focus improvement teams and other stakeholders on the results to be achieved during a specific time period, typically 90 days, to help move toward the desired future state. Goals are written to include a desired change in the current value stream plus a purpose for that change that defines an impact on how the value stream performs. Project goals also identify the person who will be responsible for seeing that the goal is achieved (the goal owner), other stakeholders or resources needed to achieve the goal (the resources), and targets for impact and timing.

Project master schedule: A plan that combines all the project goals (and sometimes their associated action plans) for a project cycle (typically 90 days). Plans are often written in the form of Gantt charts so that their progress can be easily tracked.

Project tracking center: A wall or board used to display information related to a value-stream improvement project. Typical elements include current-state and future-state maps, project implementation plan, review responsibility and countermeasure sheets, and value-stream in-process and output/outcome measures.

Reviews/checks: Regular sessions scheduled to review/confirm progress, identify problems and countermeasures, and enhance project communication. Reviews are formal sessions that typically include leadership and are scheduled on a monthly or six-week basis. Checks are informal sessions (sometimes in the form of walkthroughs) that typically occur on a daily or weekly basis. Checks typically include improvement team members and other stakeholders involved in the improvement efforts but not leadership.

Scoping: Scoping is the process of narrowing the focus of an organizational improvement effort to determine specifically which process(es) will be targeted for improvement and what improvements are desired. The lean value proposition is the format used to capture this information.

Socialization: Sometimes called "vetting" or nemawashi, socialization is a process for building consensus around a problem, a problem definition, or a proposed plan for addressing a problem. It involves presenting draft versions of the idea to be socialized to individuals and groups to gather their ideas and get them personally vested in working together. Socialization typically involves multiple cycles. Each new version of the original idea or plan needs to be shared with those who have had input into the changes until there is consensus (or at least a strong "agree to proceed/support").

Value proposition: A document created as the product of a scoping effort. It identifies the process to be targeted, the process beginning and ending points (including what's "in scope" and "out of scope"), what improvements are desired, and other information that defines the project. Along with the problem statement, it authorizes the stakeholders who will be pulled into the project to create the current- and future-state value-stream maps as well as additional stakeholders who will drive the implementation of the future state.

Value-stream map: A simple visual tool that represents what's going on in a value stream in terms of workflow, product or service transformation, and information movement. It visually tells the story of how well the value stream really works now (current state) or how the value stream might work if it were improved or redesigned (future state).

Time and Quality

Delay time (D/T): Any delay of the work of a process, including delays occurring during the work process, as well as delays occurring between processes. Examples include waiting for a call back or a form sitting in an inbox with no action being taken.

Leadtime (L/T): The total time is takes to complete a process or a process step. Leadtime consists of the combined total of process time and delay time (L/T = P/T + D/T). In terms of the patient experience, leadtime is the equivalent of the patient length of stay (LOS) for a given process.

Process time (P/T): The time it takes to actually do the work within a process, i.e., "hands on time."

Percent complete and accurate (%CA): The percentage of time that work coming into a process is what is needed to complete the work or the composite percentage of time work occurring during a process can be initiated without having to do rework or correction.

Tools/Concepts Used in Improvement Projects

Colocation: Physically grouping together workers who perform different activities so that the activities can be performed simultaneously and duplication can be eliminated. For example, colocation of registration and triage personnel is sometimes used to eliminate duplication of information requested of patients in the ED.

Continuous flow: The design and function of a work process that enables the work to move predictably through the process with no delays between processes or during an individual process.

Leveling: Adjusting the way the work is performed to meet variations in customer demand. Leveling when applied to a healthcare unit or department can mean reallocating personnel, treatment rooms, or other resources when demand varies—for example, using one staffing pattern in the morning and a different pattern in the late afternoon and evenings.

Quality at the source: Designing work and workflow in a way that ensures that errors are not allowed to be passed downstream.

Service-level agreement (SLA): An agreement between a customer and supplier process to meet certain targets, including targets for timing. Examples of internal and external SLAs are as follows: Radiology agrees to a one-hour turnaround time for all standard chest film requests from the ED (internal) and the ED agrees that all patients will be seen by a provider within 10 minutes of arrival to the ED (external).

Signaling system: A method for indicating to an upstream step that the downstream step is ready to receive new work. Updating whiteboards, using walkie-talkies, placing clipboards in a particular rack are typical signaling methods on a floor or in a department.

Standardized work: Developing and using standards or specifications for performing the work in a process, process step, or procedure according to the currently documented best method. Using standard work ensures that work is done correctly and with the least amount of waste, regardless of who is doing the work.

Visual management: Using visual controls and visual displays to manage the flow of work in a process or in the entire value stream. Visual controls—which control or guide the activity of staff, patients, or other people in the hospital—include options such as color-coded pathways to direct people to different locations or to prioritize work. Visual displays —which are tools for displaying and updating information—include items such as a project tracking board with monthly data on the average length of stay in a specific unit.

Value-Stream Improvement Roles

Stakeholders: Individuals who have a stake in seeing the value stream improved/the project succeed. This group typically includes, but is not limited to, people who work in the process as well as customer and suppliers of the value stream.

See pages 149–150 for detailed descriptions of other value-stream improvement roles.

Value-Stream Maps

Icons: The symbols used to draw a current-state or future-state value-stream map.

Inbox delay: A delay in a process that occurs when the work in progress is ready to be performed but must wait until the person or group who is to perform that work can begin (i.e., the work is ready but the people or resource that do the work are not). Inbox delays are indicated on a value-stream map with the "inbox" icon.

Information flow: The pattern of information flowing to and from a process (i.e., outside the process itself), documenting either a request for information not currently available but needed by the process or the supply of information supplied in response to a previous request (e.g., a request for Lab or Radiology results or the results supplied in response to the request). Information flow can be electronic (shown by a jagged arrow) or paper (shown by a solid arrow) flow. The specific type of information requested or supplied should always be labeled.

Other (or pure) delay: Any delay in a process that occurs once the work in the process has begun, such as waiting for a signature. "Other" delays are indicated on a value-stream map with a clock icon.

Process box: An icon used to show each major step in the process.

Process data box: An icon (symbol) used on a value-stream map to show process time, delay time and percent complete and accurate for each process in the value stream. Data boxes also can include other types of data collected, depending on what you are choosing to measure in order to better understand what's going on in a particular process.

Timeline and summary statistics (value-stream metrics): These elements include process time and leadtime totals and cumulative percent complete and accurate for entire value stream and any other data you are measuring for the value stream. (Process time and leadtime are calculated by adding up the process times and delay times for each process in the value stream. The cumulative percent complete and accurate is calculated by multiplying the percent complete and accurate metrics for all processes in the value stream. The result is a statement of probability about the chances that a given piece of work can go all the way through the system without any rework or workarounds.)

Work

Incidental work: Work that customers don't need to meet their requirements but is necessary to complete the value-creating work. For example, restocking a supply cart does not directly deliver value to patients but it is necessary for staff to be able to perform the work that does create value.

Value-creating work: Work that customers need to meet their requirements.

Waste: Anything other than the minimum amount of equipment, materials, space, and worker time and effort necessary to add value to the product or service.

About the Authors

Judy Worth

Judy, a full-time consultant based in Lexington, KY, is a partner in Lean Transformations Group and co-owner of Verble, Worth & Verble. Her practice focuses on organizational development and instructional design. During her career she has worked extensively in a variety of healthcare settings. Judy spent five years as materials developer for the Kellogg-funded Computerized Office Record Review Recertification Project for the American Board of Family Medicine. She has more than 20 years of experience as consultant and trainer for many of the federally designated organ and tissue procurement organizations in the United States, and for the past seven years she has worked as a consultant and trainer for the Organ Donation and Transplant Division of the United Kingdom National Health Service, helping it develop UK-wide systems for organ donation and apply/adapt relevant best practices from the U.S. Breakthrough Collaborative on Organ and Tissue Donation. Judy began her lean journey seven years ago when she provided the instructional design for *Mapping to See: A Value Stream Improvement Kit for the Office and Services*, published by the Lean Enterprise Institute. Since then she has cofacilitated value-stream improvement initiatives in multiple healthcare and other organizations and provided train-the-trainer development for in-house facilitators. Judy holds a BA from Harding College and an MA in Curriculum and Instruction from the University of Kentucky.

Tom Shuker

Tom, a partner in Lean Transformations Group, is a 30-year veteran in various manufacturing environments within General Motors Corp. Tom also spent two years at New United Motors Manufacturing Inc. (NUMMI), the GM-Toyota joint venture, working within the Toyota Manufacturing System and performing lean assessments of Toyota facilities in Kentucky and Japan. He has coauthored two books on lean, *Value Stream Management* and *Value Stream Management for the Lean Office*, both published by Productivity Press Inc. Tom also is a coauthor of *Mapping to See: A Value-Stream Improvement Kit for Office and Service*. Tom is also a member of an investment group that purchases small manufacturing firms. As part of this, Tom acted as CEO to guide a Wisconsin firm through a lean transformation, resulting in a remarkable competitive turnaround. Tom is especially energetic in promoting the application of lean principles and tools in nonmanufacturing environments, including healthcare (St Mary's Health Systems, Mayo Clinic, Michigan Hospital Association—Keystone Collaborative), government (City of Grand Rapids, State of Indiana), and financial services (GMAC, Capital One, Vanguard Financial). Tom has a Bachelor of Science degree from Michigan State University and an MBA from Western Michigan University.

Beau Keyte

Beau began his lean consulting career in the mid-1980s in the automotive industry, transitioned to adapting lean techniques to service and administrative processes in 1992, and has since progressed from implementing tools and techniques to developing and teaching the kind of self-sufficient thinking that challenges work and management processes, improves organizational performance and alignment, and sustains culture change. He now spends half of his time in the healthcare arena where he is designing new ways for organizations to engage, learn, grow, and succeed. In addition to assisting companies in implementing lean strategies, he also trains organizations in a variety of public and private settings. He is currently partner in the Lean Transformations Group and a faculty member and instructor for curricula at the Lean Enterprise Institute, the University of Michigan, and The Ohio State University. Beau is the coauthor of a number of journal articles and the Shingo-prize winning book *The Complete Lean Enterprise: Value Stream Mapping for Office and Administrative Processes*. He also is coauthor of *Mapping to See: A Value-Stream Improvement Kit for Office and Service*. Beau holds BSE and MBA degrees from the University of Michigan.

Karl Ohaus

In a 30-year professional career Karl has succeeded as a design engineer, inventor, company president, and consultant. This diverse background provides a unique perspective on the application of lean tools and techniques to help clients create process flow and improve performance. As a company president, he led the lean transformation of an automotive parts supplier. His coaching stresses the importance of management development and employee engagement for a successful change to a lean enterprise. In addition to his work with manufacturing, Karl has had a successful career consulting to the healthcare industry nationally and globally. In that work he has demonstrated the ability to understand and connect with doctors, nurses, and administrators and the passion that they bring to their mission, and has found it particularly rewarding. Karl is a partner in the Lean Transformations Group. He holds a BS in Mechanical Engineering from Duke University.

Jim Luckman

Jim has had the unique experience of leading three separate lean transformations: as a plant manager, as a director of a research and development center, and as a CEO of a small startup company. During these contrasting leadership roles, Jim realized that an effective lean transformation required understanding how to manage knowledge creation and how to lead for maximizing engagement and organizational creativity. Lean leaders must practice these behaviors in order to develop the environment for problem solving and learning by all the people in the organization. Jim has consolidated his personal experiences and is now helping clients see a more complete picture of what is required to lead a lean transformation. Jim is the past president and CEO of iPower Technologies, a company serving the distributed generation market of electrical power. He has 34 years of experience working in the auto industry at Delphi Automotive (formerly part of General Motors). He held several positions as chief engineer for engine components. Today, Jim is focusing his efforts on leadership coaching, application of lean in R&D, and application of lean to software development. A partner in the Lean Transformations Group, he currently coaches companies interested in companywide lean transformation and often is asked to reengage companies that have seen a decline in their lean efforts. Jim holds a BS from Tri State University in Electrical Engineering and an MS in computer engineering from Case Western Reserve University.

David Verble

David has been a performance improvement consultant and leadership coach since 2000. Prior to that, he worked for Toyota in North America for 14 years, first as an internal change agent and later as a manager of human resource development at the plant and North American levels. He has been on the workshop faculty of the Lean Enterprise Institute for eight years and has done presentations and workshops to support a number of the LEI affiliates in the Lean Global Network. David is a partner in the Lean Transformations Group and is based in Lexington, KY, where he works through Verble, Worth & Verble. He has worked with clients in manufacturing, healthcare, finance, and higher education in North America, Europe, Asia, and Australia. His work has focused on supporting clients in process improvement, development of lean management systems and practices, strategic thinking and problem solving, and leadership coaching for managers and executives. He has a graduate degree in instructional systems and performance technology and training in consulting psychology. David's primary experience in healthcare has been an eight-year relationship with a hospital in Canada. His other work in healthcare has included projects at Mayo Clinic and University of Michigan Health System.

Kirk Paluska

Kirk has held operations management positions in both high-tech manufacturing and service companies, including National Semiconductor, JDS Uniphase, and Enservio. Kirk has led lean deployments as well as the development of right-sized IT systems in service, healthcare, and manufacturing. He also was a consultant with the TWI Network and Lean Transformations Group where he helped a variety of companies incorporate lean thinking into their frontline operations, back offices, and management systems. Kirk is a faculty member of the Lean Enterprise Institute. He is a codeveloper of the Transformational Leadership workshop and a coauthor of *Mapping to See: A Value-Stream Improvement Kit for Office and Service*. Kirk has an MBA in Operations and Accounting from the University of Michigan and a BS in Electrical Engineering from Swarthmore College.

Todd Nickel

Todd has more than 15 years of experience leading continuous improvement in the food, automotive, and healthcare industries. Todd began his career as an industrial engineer, expanding responsibilities to include production supervision, operations management, and continuous improvement management within the automotive and food industries. This diverse experience and hands on implementation have allowed Todd the ability to reach sustainability through floor-level engagement and the development of problem solving at all levels of the organization. In addition to work in manufacturing, Todd has consulted with organizations seeking to implement continuous improvement formore than 10 years, including healthcare work in pharmacy, sterile processing, and laboratory operations. Todd has acted as the primary lean training provider for Michigan Technical Education Center in Southwest Michigan since 2002. Todd received a Bachelor of Science in Industrial Engineering from Western Michigan University.

The authors of *Perfecting Patient Journeys* are or have been partners or associates of the Lean Transformations Group. To learn more about their work, go to *lean-transform.com*.

Lean Enterprise Institute

The Lean Enterprise Institute (LEI) is a nonprofit learning and sharing organization with the goal of spreading lean thinking and practice throughout the world. We learn, share, and collaborate about lean through a variety of activities.

Learning Materials

We publish high-caliber books on lean thinking and practice, leadership, and management. They draw on years of research and real-world experiences from lean transformations in different organizations to provide tools that you can put to work immediately.

Education

We offer public workshops held throughout the United States, at your organization, or online, for leaders and change agents across all levels of lean experience. Our workshops are taught by thought leaders with decades of practical experience and offer you tools you can apply immediately for your own lean transformation.

Events

Every March the Lean Transformation Summit explores the latest lean concepts and case studies, presented by executives and implementers. Other events focus on an issue or industry, such as starting a lean transformation or implementing lean in healthcare.

lean.org

A quick and secure sign-up delivers these learning resources:

- John Shook's thought-leading e-letter delivered to your inbox

- Entry to a range of Forums where you can ask questions or help others

- Access to LEI case studies, articles, webinars, and interviews

About the Healthcare Value Network

In partnership with the ThedaCare Center for Healthcare Value, LEI helped establish the Healthcare Value Network to help fundamentally improve healthcare delivery through the application of lean concepts. Network member organizations learn from their peers through participation in learning and sharing opportunities. These activities include on-site visits, sharing on a collaborative private website, participation in affinity groups, and attending the annual Lean Healthcare Transformation Summit. To learn more about the Network, visit: *healthcarevalueleaders.org*

The ThedaCare Center for Healthcare Value, our partner in creating the Network, strives to create a healthcare marketplace that rewards providers for delivering value. In order to do so, the Center is a resource hub that brings together in one place the important insights, examples and worthy experiments from across health care. To learn more about the Center, visit: *createvalue.org*